THE EXCHANGE: A NOVEL

NADIJA MUJAGIC

PIONEER
PUBLISHING

CHAPTER ONE

NOW

I drive Jake to the community pool a few blocks away from our house. It's a hot day, and it's the only place I can come up with. Gallup doesn't have many community pools or lakes or ponds to cool off in, especially ones that are suitable for a four-year-old. The heat is oppressive, and the grass looks yellow and unredeemable. A perfect day for a swim and splash. When we arrive, the pool is packed and it looks like everyone is elbow-to-elbow. At least the chairs are still available for rental, so I count myself lucky. I pay for my chair, and Jake runs to the pool and jumps in.

I lie down on my rented chair and put my straw hat on. The sun's rays burn my skin but I enjoy it even though I suspect I will pay for it in blisters later. I keep my eyes trained in Jake's direction. He's a fast swimmer, and so it feels like I have to watch all the pool at once. The children scream in their playfulness, and I can feel my eyelids growing heavy. Minutes pass, but I don't have a clue how many. Children keep screaming and I jump as I open my eyes, cringing at their high-pitch voices. How had I allowed myself to close my eyes?

Jake's voice, if he is screaming, is subdued by the others.

Jake.

Where is he? I should check in on him. I look after him often to prove to myself I am a decent mother.

I remove my hat and sit up. I scan around the pool for Jake, but he's nowhere to be found. At one point, all the children resemble each other with wet hair glued to their skulls, and spotting him is impossible. I stand up and walk to the pool to get a better vantage point. I move closer to the edge, looking for Jake, but I don't see him.

This is not like Jake—even though he's only four, he's mature beyond his age, and he'd do nothing stupid. I feel lucky that he always obeys me and never questions me. He's an easy and amendable child.

After I've inspected the entire pool, my throat closes, and everything starts to spin. I'm feeling dizzy and feeling my eyes rolling in the sockets. I'm doing my best to say something, make a move, but I stare at one spot and stand in one place. Where is he?

"Jake!" My voice travels along the pool, muffled by the children's yelps. "Jake!" I scream a little harder and feel the weight of all those eyes staring at me.

"Jake! Jake, where are you?"

The lifeguard jumps from the watching platform and runs up to me. "Ma'am, you're looking for someone?"

"Yes. I'm looking for my son, Jake. I can't find him." I

extend my arms toward the pool as if I am about to dive in. "Please. Please find him." I'm on the edge of sobbing, but I try to keep my cool.

The lifeguard walks up to a megaphone and places it on his lips. "Jake! Jake, come out of the pool right now!" The children pause for a second and stare in the lifeguard's direction, but none even flinch. Then the commotion continues as if nothing is going on. "Will Jake come out of the pool now? Jake, please come out of the pool." The voice is loud and clear. But no Jake shows up.

I am picturing Jake lying on the bottom of the pool lifeless, staring at the sky with his big blue eyes. Feeling nauseas, I'm stumbling around the edge of the pool. I'm choking. With both hands on my mouth, I am shocked and alarmed, and I don't understand where Jake can be. I yell out his name twice for good measure, but my voice sounds shaky.

"Everybody, come out of the pool. Right now!" The lifeguard's voice through the megaphone dominates the block. I didn't mean to cause all this commotion, but the situation is dire. "Come out of the pool right now!"

The children line up and then inch toward the exit, some stumbling as they attempt to move faster than their legs can carry them. I stand there and watch them pushing each other and exchanging mean looks, angry about the interruption of their play.

Several minutes pass until the pool is empty. Some people gather their kids and leave while others stand by the pool wondering what's happening and waiting to see what will transpire in the next few minutes.

A large man in swimming trunks comes out of the

building next to the pool and calls for the lifeguard to jump in. "Scott, look for him inside."

Scott jumps in the pool and swims at the bottom. Both men search for Jake, one inside the pool and the other above, but I hear no reassuring words. No "here he is," or "found him.".

The lifeguard resurfaces from the bottom of the pool a few minutes later and announces, "I see nothing. I searched the entire pool."

I can't move. Reality is setting in. Jake is lost. Or kidnapped. Or had he ran away? No, no. He couldn't have run away. He is a good boy and he would never do such a thing. Good and obedient. A mama's boy. A little angel. How can I lose him like this? I haven't been the best mother, I admit, but the thought of a missing Jake over-whelms me.

The large man approaches me. "Ma'am, we did our due diligence to find your son, but he doesn't appear to be here. I'm sorry." I notice gloom in his eyes. "Are you sure he was in the pool last?"

"Yes, yes, he was in the pool last." I say. Tears are filling my eyes. I cannot stop them.

"Is it possible he came out of the pool and left?"

"It's possible, but that's not Jake-like. He would come right to me if he was tired of swimming." I look around, expecting to see Jake any second.

"I'm very sorry, but there's nothing more we can do. If you're certain that he's missing, call the police." He places his hand on my shoulder. I feel its weight. "Do you want us to call the cops for you?"

The pool looks empty and as smooth as glass. The floor of the pool can now be seen, covered in blue tiles. It is as crystal clear as the fact that Jake is nowhere to be found.

I stand motionless and let the sun blind my eyes from the reflection of the pool.

"No, no. I'll call." In my mind, I choose to drive to the police station instead. I don't trust phones.

My head is spinning. I clench my fists. Jake's voice is echoing in my ears, "Mommy, I'm here. Come get me."

But when the large man taps me on the shoulder to tell me the pool is closing for the day and I need to leave, I realize Jake's voice is just a delusion.

Only one thought crosses my mind. Corey. It must be Corey who kidnapped Jake.

CHAPTER TWO

FOUR YEARS EARLIER

"I can't believe you're leaving. And tomorrow, no less." My friend Michelle said with a sad expression on her face. She swirled her long hair with a left pinky while holding a cup in her other hand and sipping her soda through a straw. We were sitting in our favorite diner in Gallup. It was a Tuesday morning, and neither one of us had anything better to do. We'd both graduated from high school the year prior and skipped college like most people our age did in our small town.

I shrugged. "Well, doesn't hurt to try. Plus, I'm meeting with an agent the day after I arrive."

"You're not scared?"

"Scared of what?" I pitched my voice high.

"Aren't there, like, many homeless in L.A.?"

"Yeah. So?"

"Isn't there a high crime rate where all homeless people are?"

I waved my hand at her. "Oh, shush. It's not like I'm gonna hang out with them, you know."

"That's not the point, Sam. You don't know the city well. It can eat you alive."

"Shell." She hated it when I called her Shell. "You don't know what you're talking about."

She smirked and took another sip of her soda. She slammed the glass against the table—and then crunched up her nose. "Have you ever been?"

"No." I said, expecting another wave of barrage.

"Honestly, Sam, sounds like you don't know what you're talking about."

"I'm not afraid." I said.

She widened her eyes and leaned on the chair cushion behind her.

"That's good!" She looked out the window, squinting her eyes.

I sensed nostalgia in them, a longing for a change, perhaps. The town we grew up in was a vacuum—it sucked the life out of people.

I'd known Michelle for so long that I no longer remembered where or when we met. Over the years, she'd become my one and only genuine friend. Unassuming, shy, emphatic, Michelle was what I looked for in a person. We spent a crazy amount of time together when growing up. I could never admit to my mother that Michelle was the only person I trusted and loved. Even if I tried, I couldn't twist this truth. Both being only children in our nuclear families, Michelle and I bonded like sisters.

She turned around and, with high enthusiasm, continued, "Wouldn't it be cool to meet Brad Pitt or Matt Damon and hang out with them?"

I laughed. "Yes. Yes, it would."

She swirled the straw around the glass. "I'm proud of you, Sam. I wouldn't have guts to leave the town."

"Will you come visit me?" I wanted to change the tone of our conversation. So far, it sounded too negative for my liking.

"Are you kiddin' me? Of course, I'm coming to visit you. Just say when." I doubted her parents would let her.

"Cool."

"Did you find a place to live, or are you just going to wing it when you get there?"

"I found an apartment on Craigslist. It was easier than I thought."

"Great." I could sense envy on her smile as her lips danced in a funny way. I knew Michelle well. Like the fact that she often got depressed and wished to uproot her life and go elsewhere to find happiness. She hid her feelings well from the others, but not from me. "Sounds like you're on your way."

"I can't wait." I said. It was true. I couldn't wait to get out of here. I had dreams to pursue that I couldn't even fathom pursuing in this town.

"You'll do great. You're a talented actress. Can you do a Phoebe for me?" Michelle loved the show Friends.

Impersonation was my forte. I transformed into Phoebe and spoke the lines from one episode, singing the smelly cat song the character was so famous for, sending Michelle into a hysterical laugh.

"Oh, my goodness, that is so good!" She wiped tears from her eyes. Once we'd caught our breath after laughing, she said, "I'm going to miss you. What's your mom saying about you leaving?"

"Nothin'," I said.

"Really? Nothing? I'd imagine she'd be a nervous wreck. I mean, all she does is talk about you, whether she's alone or with you. You're her world."

"I know. She'll manage," I said.

"I guess. It's not like, you're five million miles away," she added a nervous laugh. "You can always come back home."

I nodded, though I couldn't have disagreed more. I'd rather eat broken glass for lunch every day than return to this shithole. Michelle kept smiling, but her eyes gave away sadness. When we were in high school, she had bouts of depression and wouldn't leave the house for days. While my mother let me wander around the town as I wished, her parents controlled her every step. One time, when she got a C on an essay, her parents grounded her for two weeks. They hired a private tutor and made her write two essays a day until she perfected them. Michelle tried to convince me they did this for her own good, but I knew otherwise. Her parents were sadistic, ego-driven assholes I wanted to smack every time I saw them. But I played nice.

Silence ensued, and we both got lost in our own thoughts for a few seconds. The smell of the eggs and sausage was wafting through the diner. The customers were arriving, as the lunch hour ushered them inside to find food.

Michelle stared at the people as they walked by our table. Gossiping was common in our town—it kept us all alive and entertained. She turned to me and said, "Oh, did you hear Steve is enrolling in the police academy?"

Steve was our mutual friend. Everyone knew he had a crush on me while we were in high school. He showed his interest in me by sitting at the same table in the school cafeteria and asking me the dumbest questions. Steve wasn't the brightest, and I couldn't stand a thought of dating him. I sensed Michelle liked him with her frequent mention of him in passing.

My interest in boys was subdued by my focus to explore other things in life, such as acting. But Steve remained a good friend. If I ever asked him for help with anything under the sun, he would be there for me in a heartbeat.

"Really?" I sounded surprised even though Steve had told me, boasting with pride.

Michelle nodded. "It'll be nice to have a cop we know well in the neighborhood. It just feels safer."

I gave her a vague smiled and said nothing.

Michelle tapped her palms on the table. "Let's do something fun today. Shall we?"

I was going to say no at first, because of my trip jitters, but then I realized I'd already packed my single suitcase, and I was ready to go. My bus didn't leave until noon the following day. There was plenty of time to feel the town, to rummage around it, and to remind myself why I was leaving.

"Like what?"

"Have you heard of Bikram yoga?"

"I've heard of yoga, but the Bikram part doesn't ring a bell."

Michelle laughed. "It's like regular yoga, except you do

it in a boiling room and you sweat bullets while you're doing it."

"Eww! But that seems fun. Let's do it." We both got up from the table and headed for the door. As I stood next to Michelle, I towered over her. She'd always been much shorter than me. I placed my hand on her shoulder, already missing her. We found ourselves outside and embraced the fresh Gallup air.

In twenty-four hours, I would erase it from my lungs.

CHAPTER THREE

Yah-ta-hey was the name of the town I grew up in. It was a place where distant dogs barked in the mornings and crickets chirped at night—and nothing else. The name meant "like a devil" in Navajo, an unusual choice given the clusters of churches in the town and nearby. It was a place where secrets were held deep.

Our house was set far back from the main road, surrounded by acres of flat land. The nearby houses were distant enough for privacy, but the sound traveled fast and far throughout our small neighborhood. We knew everyone. The town had a population of six hundred people, occupying four square miles. To get any business done, you'd need to go to the closest large city nearby, which was Gallup, approximately eight miles down south. But even Gallup seemed a bit cramped, having more churches per capita than any other known city in America. Or that was what I thought, anyway.

My grandfather, Cliff Crawford, bought the house just after World War II. It was big enough to house two small families. When my father, Bill short for William, married my mother Mary, they succumbed to the idea of living there for its simplicity. My grandparents died at a young age unexpectedly within a couple of weeks of each other —my grandmother first of kidney failure, then my grandfather of a heart attack. My father was mourning, though he told us one day he wasn't too surprised given their insistence on using alternate medicine to treat their illnesses.

My maternal grandparents died at a young age, too. I hadn't been lucky enough to meet them. My mother mentioned them once or twice with a great sense of dread and hesitation, and her lack of sharing discouraged me from asking more.

My paternal grandparents were all I knew.

I was four years old when they both died. We buried Grandmother in the main Gallup cemetery. Her casket was sitting next to the hole, surrounded by hundreds of people, almost everyone who lived in Yah-ta-hey. My parents and my grandfather were in the front row. I was perched between my parents, holding their hand. We had no clue Grandfather would come next, just a short two weeks after we buried Grandmother. The place he stood during the funeral was his burial spot two days after he died.

Father didn't cry, which surprised me. Mother shed a few tears at the funerals, but she, too, seemed distant and emotionless. I followed suit and suppressed my crying, thinking my Grandparents were waiting for us at home; Grandmother cooking in the kitchen and Grandfather caring for the vegetable garden in their backyard. I couldn't quite comprehend what dying was all about until I realized neither one was ever going to cross the house threshold again.

Father was more concerned about the cost of the funerals than anything, even though he was now the sole owner of the house. My grandparents paid off the mortgage long ago, so we lived there for free. The house was rackety and old. The floor in the kitchen wasn't level, so my mother complained how uncomfortable and dizzy it made her being there. My room was on the second floor, and I'd often spend time there in dead silence. Michelle would come visit when her mother felt like driving a few minutes down the road. She was the only child in my neighborhood willing to come to our house and the only one I wanted to visit. We'd play hide and seek, often venturing into the creepiest part of the house—our unfinished basement. Its size was impressively large, yet its functions limited. In one corner was an old washer hanging by its efficiency thread. The low ceilings gave the space a claustrophobic feel, but us girls didn't mind. We were short back then.

After my grandparents died, Father turned into a nasty creature. He acted strange, often coming home late and screaming at Mother. She was quiet, refusing to respond to his insults. She kept them close to herself, protecting me from the monster my father had become. He distanced himself from us, often pretending we weren't in his presence. He had no smile or kind words for me anymore. I blamed myself for Father's turn of character, but my mother would whisper in my ear and assure me, "It's not your fault, love. Not your fault."

My mother's attempt at love balanced off my father's complete lack of it. She called me different names often, such as a jewel, a rare pearl, a diamond. All those gems flattered me until that thing I did that shook me to my core.

After that, I no longer deserved to be called those names.

The next person in our family to die was my father, Bill. Almost two years after my grandparents died. I was six years old. He was twenty something. I didn't even know his age. He didn't die of a heart attack or a kidney failure. Besides being angry all the time, and grumpiness eating at him, he was quite a healthy man. Every morning, he'd grab an apple from a bowl sitting on the kitchen counter and he'd crunch it away. Eating and treating his body well were his priority in life. But no one knew except for me the bad thing I did. Even to this day, no one knows.

But what I did was unintentional. A mistake. I later learned that accidental murder was called manslaughter, and that wasn't actual murder. I kept saying that to myself.

It was the fear of knowing how easy it was to erase someone's life. In a matter of mere minutes. Any gem of the world couldn't encounter the amount of guilt and remorse I felt. But I had to keep the secret from my mother. From Michelle. From this town.

From me.

CHAPTER FOUR

My name is Sam, short for Samantha. Last name Crawford. My grandmother once told me Samantha meant "name of God," or "God has heard," but it also meant a flower or a blossom. Some people, before they saw me, mistook me for Samuel, but it didn't matter since both names meant the same.

My mother raised me to be a girly girl, wearing pink dresses and leather shoes. On Sundays, we'd show up at the church and she would glow, showing me off as a trophy. As I grew older, I learned my mother was as complex as a Diophantine equation. On the outside, she looked like a toughest nut to crack. She took a great deal of time to care for herself. Her skin was smooth as milk. She ironed her clothes to crispness. Her makeup was impeccable and her jewelry matched it. Next to her, my father looked like a lumberjack: his hair dirty and disheveled, his shirt untucked; boots covered in dirt. The two were the complete opposite.

Mother knew what to do and what to say to people

most of the time. Her charm was her signature, though it seemed to fade away when she and Father took to fighting all the time.

On the inside, my mother held a different story. Months after Father died, she stopped getting up in the mornings. She stopped wanting to leave the house or even look in the mirror until she'd guzzled those shiny-white pills. Even though Father was no longer around to keep ruining her life, she told me she could still hear his voice insulting her, abusing her with the most despicable words. She got sadder and thinner, and the more pills she took, the more she faded away and forgot to do all the important things. Then she went away for a month—rehab, I was told—and a month felt like an eternity to my six-year-old mind.

Mother returned with renewed hope that the rehab had cured her for good. Her visits to Church increased in frequency and she often preached to me at home, telling me that God had heard her prayers. She'd be well for days at a time until the slightest commotion shook her dignity. Then she'd spiral down again to rock bottom. I wanted to help Mother, but all I could think about was what I'd done. I'd caused her pain. Ruined her life. So instead of reaching out to her, I fled from her instead, as soon as I was able.

Leaving town and venturing to other parts of the country took bold courage. There was no collective wisdom to guide me. The day I told my mother I was leaving for L.A., she burst into tears. I sat next to her and waited for her to calm down.

"Mom, come on, you knew this was coming." When I said those words, another wave of sobbing came. I scoffed.

"Mom, please stop. I have less than a week to get ready. I can't deal with this crap now."

By "get ready," I meant sending out emails to as many agents as possible. She looked at me through tears, wiping them at once. I felt nothing.

"I can't believe my baby is moving away."

"Why can't you believe it?"

"Are you moving because of me?"

My mother's guilt seeped from every edge of her, but I couldn't let it get to me. I had too much guilt of my own.

"No, Mom. I'll be in touch all the time." I lied to keep her quiet.

"You will?"

"Yes." I raised my voice. "God, why do you always need to be so dramatic?"

My mother and I had grown apart over years. I didn't intend for that to happen. It just did. Every step she made closer to me, I made one farther from her. We never touched, embraced, felt one another. I realized it suited me that way, because I gained the independence I always craved for. My mother lived her own life while I lived mine.

"There's no drama. I'm just going to miss you, darling." My mother's voice was soft. She looked different without makeup. She looked unsightly while being sad. I should have told her to pull herself together, but I didn't. I couldn't look at her anymore, so I stormed out of our apartment for a walk.

When Father died, Mother couldn't stand living in the large house. She thought the ghosts were inside and she didn't like being watched. She found a small apartment in the heart of Gallup and had us both move there while she rented the house out to a family of four. Later I surmised her real motive was to save some money and use any rent income leftover on her drugs. I hated how selfish she'd become, but I didn't have a voice in our household. I just existed.

I could barely wait to move out of our apartment. L.A. was calling me to my new home.

The morning I left, my mother gave me a ride in her beat-up Jeep. She'd never quite learned to take her car for maintenance. Parts would fall down on the road as she drove. Throughout the years, none of her short-term boyfriends dared to get close to her and be a kind of man to help with such tasks. And yet, she believed in love. She believed in God. Drugs and God didn't go well for most people, but to my mother, they did. When she stayed away from drugs, she thanked God for the strength; and when she was high... well, she also thanked God for it.

At the bus station, I gave Mother a quick hug and turned around to board the bus. She mumbled something about visiting L.A. soon, or something along those lines, but I didn't acknowledge it. I found my seat and buried my head in a magazine. In the corner of my eye, I saw Mother standing outside, but I didn't bother to look up or wave like they did in movies. I imagined her saying prayers under her breath, asking God to save me from the devil.

CHAPTER FIVE

The bus arrived in L.A. around midnight. It dropped us off at the Union station, an enormous building in the city's heart. I pin-dropped my new home on the map of my phone, some twelve miles away in North Hollywood. As I shuffled across the bus platform, a strange feeling over-came me, like it always did when I found myself in a new place. I seemed to have tamed my anxiety mostly over the years, but it always peeked its ugly head out in new situa-tions. People and voices haunted me.

Like that time, my father appeared out of nowhere, sitting on my bed, looking at me and smiling. It happened about a year after he died. His appearances quietened my guilt on such occasions. It meant he was still alive, albeit untouchable. I broke the news to my mother that Dad visited me. In return, she narrowed her eyes and the same day took me to a psych ward for investigation. They kept me there for a week. The chief psychologist there diag-nosed me with schizophrenia, based on his observation. A severe amount of distress caused me to hallucinate and see people and hear voices. He confirmed the diagnosis when I told him my father kept following me around the psych ward. After the psychologist prescribed me meds, my father rarely returned, but random voices occupied my head every once in a while. I cringed at sounds.

At the station, the collective voices produced a steady, loud white noise. People walked like robots and looked as if they were made of plastic, like mannequins. An older man stared at me as we walked past each other. He licked his lips, then he pursed them as if blowing me a kiss. I diverted my eyes and kept walking to the exit.

Even though it was past midnight in May, the air was hot. Summer in LA started early. I took off my fleece jacket and stood near the exit, calling for an Uber ride. In front of me was a city, lit up. They said New York City never slept, but LA had to be the next one up. Near the door, I took a copy of Metro magazine and placed it under my armpit while looking down at my phone. A bunch of little cars showed on the app, one finally confirming that it was my ride.

While waiting for my Uber ride, I grabbed the *Metro* and flipped through the pages before noticing the ads in the back. Before I left for L.A., I'd contacted a bunch of agents to represent me for acting gigs, and I squealed in joy when I heard from one. My mother had given me five thousand dollars—and God only knew where she got it from—and I had some savings of my own. But with the LA standard of living, the cash I had wouldn't stretch for long. I had to find another job.

My Uber ride showed, and I jumped into the car. I'd be home soon. The owner had mailed me the key to my studio apartment, and I rushed to reach for my pocket to double check it was still there. I felt the tip of the key and sighed with relief. Everything was going as planned. Traffic seemed heavy, but that was a usual occurrence in L.A., regardless of the time of day.

About thirty minutes later, the car pulled into a driveway and stopped in front of a five-story brick building. The street lights were off; some lights were projecting from the apartments. I stood in front of the building and studied it. It didn't look pretty or inviting, but it was my new home. A place I belonged.

CHAPTER SIX

The elevator in the five-story building of my new apartment didn't work. I swore under my breath as I dragged the luggage up the stairs, step by step. My tummy was growling from hunger and exhaustion was setting in. I was too tired to examine the building carefully, but the brown wallpaper made me nauseous. The neon lights in the ceiling were flickering and making a buzzing noise. As I advanced up the stairs, different smells converged, but the smell of weed dominated. It could be a perfect setting for a horror movie, I thought. Breathing heavily through my mouth, I went through a heavy metal door on the fourth floor and entered the hallway where my apartment was.

The air in my new home smelled of vomit and old socks. I gasped and blocked my nose with my fingers. There was one large window on the opposite side, and I rushed to open it before sticking my head out to breathe in some fresh air. Stars decorated the sky, and the moon gave away brightness. Just as I was about to walk away and get set, I noticed a figure in front of the building moving behind a light pole. A woman barged in on the figure and yelled something unintelligible. The figure, who appeared to be a man, lifted his arms and defended himself against the force of the woman's arms attacking him. The neighborhood definitely didn't seem as safe as Gallup.

I moved away from the window, hoping no one saw me. I turned around and studied my new home. My studio apartment didn't look special. The apartment comprised a small room, a kitchenette, and in one corner was the entrance to the bathroom. The landlord furnished it with a futon sofa, a small coffee table, a chair in one corner of the room, and a TV. As long as I had a TV, I didn't care about anything else. Before I left, Michelle was kind to give me her Netflix login. She had me swear by my mother and God I wouldn't share with anyone else, but who was she kidding? I knew nobody else. Watching movies and studying acting were my favorite pass times. It was all I did at home, all alone, when Mother was away.

I sat down and ate the trail mix my mother had prepared for my trip. She said she would have made me a sandwich, but she'd ran out of bread. The little food I had was enough to satisfy my hunger. I lay down on the sofa and looked up at the ceiling. The man's and the woman's voice outside moved to another location. All seemed to be quiet until I heard a thump. I stood up from my lying position and concentrated on the sound. Where did it come from? Then again—a loud thump. The thump turned into a continuous noise coming from upstairs. It was my neighbor above me.

I stormed outside of my apartment and headed to the next floor up. The lights in the hallway were flickering, giving off a spooky vibe. The hallway was narrow and I could touch the walls on both sides within a single reach. I climbed up the stairs and got closer to the sound source— the apartment above me. I placed my ear next to the door and heard music playing. It sounded like a bass line to a heavy metal song, deep and fast.

I paused for a second and rehearsed what I wanted to say in my head. I hoped that whatever came out of my mind would come the same way out of my mouth. Most of the time, my thoughts were scary, so I stayed silent in order not to scare anyone away. How much easier it was to pretend to be someone else. I took a breath and focused again on my reasoning. My request was simple: for my neighbor to lower the volume of their music so I could get some sleep tonight. Sitting on the bus for twelve straight hours hadn't been conducive to a sound sleep.

I mustered up the courage and knocked. The heavy bass of the music overrode the chirpy sound of my knocking. I knocked again, but no sound penetrated beyond the door. I formed my hand into a fist and banged on the door as hard as I could. The music stopped. As they got closer, the steps on the other side got louder. The door opened with mighty force and in front of me stood a man who I guessed would be in his early thirties, except his tattoos made him look older and tired. His hair was tied in dreadlocks and his nose was pierced. He looked angry.

"What do you want?" he asked.

I feared people, but over years, I'd learned to hide it well. Like now, my palms were sweating and my heart raced. But I maintained my poker face.

"Hi, I'm Sam. I'm your new downstairs neighbor." I extended my arm to shake his hand.

Instead, he measured me up and down and gave me a why-are-you-bothering-me nod.

I continued, "Hey, so, I wanted to ask you if you can turn the music down a bit. You know, I just came to town and I'm kinda tired. I need to sleep." I smiled to ease the situation, but the man kept looking at me with angry eyes. What was he so angry about?

"If you don't like it, move out." With those words, he slammed the door. I stood there motionless until the sound of music repelled and sent me where I came from. I lied down on the couch and formed myself into a ball. The sounds outside howled and screeched. My eyelids closed, and exhaustion lulled me into a deep sleep.

CHAPTER SEVEN

Sometime around three a.m., a round of gunshots woke me up. Then the screams came. I couldn't tell how close the shooting was, but I didn't dare go near the window to check it out. My heart hammering, I drew in the blanket and covered my head. I had to be living in the worst part of the city. The screaming continued until the cop's sirens came closer and then there was silence. I stayed covered like that, listening carefully and not moving an inch as if paralyzed from fear. Things didn't scare me often, but this apartment seemed to breed horror. I struggled to keep my eyes open, but they eventually gave up, and I fell asleep again.

I slept in the next morning. This apartment, this neighborhood, and this city were a stark difference from the eerie peace of Yah-ta-hey. I told myself I would be patient and get used to it. Nothing about this place seemed good and graceful. When I stood up, a sharp pain cut through my lower back. I suspected that was the work of the uncomfortable futon. I spread my legs and bent down, stretching to ease the pain.

I made my way to the window. Everything looked different in daylight. There was a park across the building with trees about to grow. A narrow road separated the park from the building, a curb only on one side. A few people walked down the sidewalk, minding their business. Everything looked peaceful, and there was no sound from my neighbor upstairs. It was as if the shooting last night had never happened.

My mouth made a wide yawn, and suddenly I craved coffee. In the kitchenette, I found some leftover coffee pods and shoved one in the coffeemaker on the counter.

I tossed around the futon, thinking about my meeting today with the agent who'd emailed me back while I was still at home. When her email arrived in my inbox, I screeched and only then believed miracles existed. Stacey Goldberg sounded enthusiastic about our potential collaboration—she pointed out she was relatively new to being an agent and was looking to build her list with new clients who were just starting out like me. Every time I'd needed a boost to feel better about myself, I'd opened up my email and read Stacey's note repeatedly.

One caveat she gave was that she could only meet me in person to discuss details. She then suggested we meet five days after, which put me in the panic mode, searching for a place to live and booking a bus ticket. Now that I'd seen the apartment, I understood why it had been available for several months. It was in a sketchy location, and neighbors didn't seem friendly. My first night proved that.

I opened my email and looked again at the name of the

diner Stacey wanted me to meet her at. My black dress was sitting across the chair armrest where I put it last night. It was the best outfit I'd brought from home. It made me look skinnier, yet elegant. I took a shower and applied make-up to my eyes and cheeks. I smiled at the image I saw in the mirror. I hoped Stacey would be satisfied with my looks, too.

As I headed out, my upstairs neighbor played loud music. I shook my head and slammed the door behind me. I took a deep breath and walked down the stairs and out of the building. The day was hot, and my black dress absorbed the sunrays. Maybe black wasn't the best choice for today's weather, but I wouldn't stay in the heat for too long. I pulled my phone and called an Uber. Once confirmed, a little car on the Uber map appeared to be a couple of blocks away. A gray Toyota sedan was approaching. Two minutes to go.

While waiting for the car to show up, my hands started to sweat and my heart beat faster. What if Stacey didn't like me? I took a deep breath and tried to think more positively. Perhaps I worried for nothing. Maybe everything would go well during our meeting.

The diner, according to the driver's GPS, was a mere fifteen minutes away. It was only eleven, but I wanted to get early and get a good seat. Getting there ahead of time and getting a feel for the place would ease my nerves.

I sat behind the driver and looked through the window, observing other cars driving in the opposite direction and the occasional passerby on the sidewalk. The driver turned the radio on. Rap music played, and he looked at me through the mirror as if he was checking my reaction. I had no time to worry about the radio. My mind focused on my meeting with Stacey.

"Everything okay?" the driver said.

"Yep." I said, trying not to prolong the conversation.

"Going on a hot date?"

I rolled my eyes. "Nope."

"Well, you look quite fancy, that's why I thought it." He smiled.

"Thanks. I'll take that as a compliment." I took my phone out and pretended I was busy texting someone.

Minutes later, my driver pulled over at a curb and announced our arrival. It was eleven forty-five—it took longer than I thought to get there. Plenty of time to sit down and calm down my nerves.

The diner looked like an abandoned train from the outside. A sign FUN RIDE DINER sat across the entire length of the restaurant. If I were choosing a meeting location, this would not be it. The exterior looked uninviting, and I'd hoped the interior would make up for it.

I walked through the door and looked to my left, then my right. The booths looked like train seats. The light was plentiful, and the waitresses walked around fast, holding plates with food. When I tried to decide on which booth to pick, I heard a call. "Sam?"

Taken by surprise, I looked around, thinking I'd misheard my name, but the same voice called it again. "Sam!" this time they sounded more confident and impatient.

At a booth on my right sat a woman in her early thirties. She had a short haircut and big brown eyes and she wore red lipstick. She waved at me and smiled.

Butterflies fluttered in my stomach as if my whole life

depended on this meeting. I walked to the booth and extended my arm. "Hi. You must be Stacey?"

She reached out and grabbed my hand. "Yes, I'm Stacey. Have a seat."

She took her hand out of mine and pointed at the seat opposite hers. When I sat down, Stacey stared at me with her enormous eyes. Did she study me? I dropped my eyes down as heat flooded to my face. I didn't know what to do or say next.

"So?" Stacey broke the silence. "You want to be an actress?"

"Yes." I said. "It's been a dream of mine since I was a little kid."

"Indeed. You certainly have the looks for it." She was holding a cup of tea with both hands, and it occurred to me she must have arrived much earlier. "Tell me. What are you hoping to get out of this relationship?" She brought the cup closer to her lips and sipped the tea.

"Um. Well."

A waitress came to our table and asked me what I wanted to order. Stacey looked at me, as if I was in some kind of test.

"I'll have a cup of coffee, please."

"Anything to eat?" The waitress asked, holding a pen and looking at the small notepad in front of her.

I looked at Stacey and she shook her head—or perhaps I imagined it—but I got a sense that this would not be a long meeting.

"No, thanks. Just coffee, please."

The waitress didn't say a word and walked away towards the kitchen.

I looked at Stacey. Her eyes looked impatient. "Go on."

"Well, I was hoping you can help me with my acting career. I need someone to represent me and help me take it off."

She tilted her head to a side as if it surprised her to hear this, like she'd just learned she was an acting agent.

"A-ha." That was all she said until she asked another question. "What will you do to convince me?" I cringed inside. Her question took me back to my math class, my least favorite, when the teacher to ask me to solve a problem on the board in front of the entire class. Even though I studied for it, I stumbled at the question.

I leaned against the seat behind me and shrugged. Her eyes rested on mine; her smile had long disappeared. I would imagine that being in this industry, your skin had to be thick to protect someone from stealing your soul. Stacey's brows furrowed. She played with her tea mug by spinning it around. Her impatience seemed to grow by the minute. My mind felt cloudy, but I wanted to leave a good impression. I had to convince her I was worth a shot.

"I'm here to talk to you about the possibility of being represented by you. And I would appreciate the gesture if you would."

Stacey widened her eyes further, if that was possible, and laughed. She sounded like a witch in a horror movie. Her eyes twinkled like stars, but malice leaked out of them.

"Let me ask you this. Did you bring any material for me to watch?"

"Material?" I asked in dismay. My throat closed and I could no longer think.

"Yes. Like sample videos of you acting. Do you have any?"

"Oh, that. No, but I could produce them soon and send them to you?"

She shook her head and placed a smile on her face, as if pleased at her discovery that I was a lost case.

"Sam. You need to know one important thing about acting in Hollywood. You either perish or persist. Understand? Perish or persist. And the way you're dealing with your business, you're well on your way to perishing."

As I watched her lips move to get those words out of her mouth, my own were agape. I wanted to believe I was in the middle of a nightmare and I'd wake up at any moment and continue a lovely conversation with my potential agent. Words escaped me and I had nothing to offer. If we played chess, this would be a definitive checkmate.

I'd lost.

Stacey placed a twenty-dollar bill on the table and tapped it twice with her fingers before she said that coffee was on her. As she stood up, she looked at me with her big brown eyes and repeated, "Perish or persist. Good luck, Sam."

Then she moved toward the exit door and disappeared into the L.A. heat.

I felt sick to my stomach and walked home. Perhaps the constant movement would shake off the feeling of pity and make me feel better.

The humidity was so high that it drenched my black dress in sweat. I walked toward my house with my head down, oblivious to the surrounding people. I reflected on the meeting. Was this the end of my career? How could I be so naïve not to have thought of material to present?

A sudden downpour disrupted my racing mind. The

rain pelted down with vengeance, and it was a great opportunity to let tears roll down my cheeks.

CHAPTER EIGHT

That dreadful afternoon, after meeting with Stacey, I took a stroll to a nearby park to clear my mind.

The park was big and empty, and the air felt warm. At the edges of the path were benches, worn out from use and the rain. I sat akimbo and closed my eyes, oblivious to my surroundings. Stacey's words echoed in my mind. With her as my only option and hope, my status as a rising actress looked grim. My mother once told me some people get luckier cards than others. Since my birth, I had been handed not one ace.

The voice above me startled me. "What are you thinking about?"

I lifted my head to see a young man whose head was covering the sun. He smiled down at me.

"Hey," I said.

"Mind if I sit next to you?"

I looked at the spot and said, "No, not at all."

He was tall with the radiating blue eyes people could encounter only in dreams.

"My name is Sebastian. But you can call me Seb."

"Oh, hi, Seb. My name is Samantha. You can call me Sam."

"Seb and Sam. That sounds nice." We both smiled at this discovery. "Do you live here, or just visiting?"

"I live around the corner. You?"

"Yeah, not too far. I moved to L.A. about a year ago. I grew up in a small Vermont town."

"It's cold up there, isn't it?"

"It sure is. My parents are French Canadian. Canadian winters are even worse."

"Do you like heat?"

He shrugged like he didn't care either way. "I don't mind it. People get used to changes, eventually. It's survival of the fittest."

"I suppose. So, what are you doing in L.A.?"

"Me? Like everyone else. I'm here to try acting."

I bubbled and propped myself up, widening my eyes. "You are?"

"Yeah, you too?" His index finger was pointing at me.

I nodded. "Yep. And how's it going so far?"

He shrugged again, but this time his shoulders looked weighed down. "Could be better." He shook his head. "I didn't realize it would be so hard."

"I'm in the same boat." It was difficult to admit that, but lying would be pointless.

"Are you auditioning?"

"Um... no. You?"

"I audition at least once a week, but I almost never get picked. I got chosen for a commercial a couple of months ago. It's not a movie, but it's something."

It was more than I could ever dream of at the moment. "What commercial?"

He laughed. "For a toothpaste. Nothing exciting."

"I disagree. It's quite exciting." I smiled.

"Have you been luckier with gigs?"

I shook my head, pursing my lips. "No. Not a thing. Though I just arrived in L.A."

"You know what?" He studied me with his penetrating eyes. "You look a little like Emma Stone. Actually, not a little. A lot like Emma Stone."

"Seriously? No one has ever told me that before."

"No? But you look a lot like her."

I shrugged, recalling the actress's facial features: the round face, the button nose, blue eyes. After a few seconds, I came to an admission. "I can see why you think that."

"I kinda wonder if Hollywood needs another Emma Stone," he said. "You know?"

My heart sunk. "What do you mean?"

"Let's face it. They won't call you if you look like a famous actress. They already have an Emma Stone. Why another?" The young man was saying all this like it was no big deal, but he was stabbing my heart. "And if they needed an Emma Stone, they'd call Emma Stone, not you. But, of course..."

"All due respect, but you don't know how this business works. You're just spewing words out, and none of it is true." I heard panic in my voice.

"Hey, hey. I didn't mean it that way." He reached out for my hand to touch it, and I moved it out of his way.

"Don't you touch me. I wish I'd never bothered talking

to you. Goodbye." I stood up and walked away from the bench.

"Sam, Sam." He called after me. "You took it all wrong. Come back. When Emma Stone dies, you'll be the one!"

The rest of his words became a blur.

CHAPTER NINE

I lay on my futon, staring at the ceiling. My phone rang. Michelle's bright face lit up my screen.

"Hello," I said. I missed Michelle. When things didn't go well for either of us, we'd find comfort in each other's company. It taught us to forget problems and shove them under the rug.

"Hey, Sam." Her voice was straining, as if it wanted to be cheerful, but it failed her. "How's it going?"

"It's going okay." I had no reservation in telling Michelle everything, but I put things into perspective. "You know, it's been only two days. I have to be patient."

"Why are you saying that?" She sounded alarmed.

"Well." I paused. I closed my eyes as if my words were about to sting. "I imagined things would be a little easier than this. People here are unforgiving."

"Why?" Michelle was always persistent. She knew what questions to ask to uncover the layers.

"I met with the agent." Silence.

"And?"

"It didn't go well. It went horribly, as a matter of fact."

"Oh, Sam. I'm so sorry. What are you going to do?"

Sometimes she asked me questions I hadn't had a chance to ponder on or formulate an answer for. Like this one.

"I... I need to find a job as soon as possible. I don't have a lot of money left. I've spent almost all I had on rent."

"That's a good idea. It will make your days go by quicker."

"How are things in Gallup?" I didn't care, but asked out of courtesy.

"Same old." Michelle laughed. "You're lucky, Sam. I wish I could go somewhere like you. I feel out of place and..."

While Michelle spoke, my attention shifted to the corner of the room where I had placed the Metro. I should comb through the ads in the back and find a suitable job.

"... well, anyway, I don't want to bore you with my problems, Sam." Michelle was finishing her sentence.

"Oh, you're not. You know what? I have to go now. Talk to you later." I blew her a kiss and hung up the phone.

I grabbed the newspaper and flipped it to the back pages to read the job ads. An auto mechanic? Nah. I possessed no technical skills. A waitress? Not my first choice. The truth of the matter is, I possessed little of any skills. When I was a teenager, I tried to get a job bagging groceries, but my mother had burned many bridges in town, so nobody wanted to give me a job, even when they felt sorry for me. It wasn't like I wouldn't work. My town was too small to forgive the imperfections in my mother who, by rumors, neglected me and loved drugs more than anything.

A particular ad drew my attention. I read it repeatedly:

SEEKING A BARISTA AT A POPULAR CAFÉ
IN L.A. WILLING TO TRAIN.
MUST APPLY IN PERSON. NO PHONE
CALLS.

The ad listed the address for Spy Café on the last line. No phone calls. Something odd rang about it, but I refused to ponder too hard. I clipped the ad and saved it for later as a reference.

An hour later, I took the stairs (the building elevator still didn't work) and headed out to find a bus that would lead me to the cafe. Thirty minutes later, I arrived. From the outside, Spy Café looked like it had just arrived from a previous century. For a popular place, as advertised, it looked unkempt and unappealing.

I entered, and the heavy scent of coffee splashed over me. A man in his fifties stood behind the counter as I entered. He did a double take and smiled. Sometimes I forgot I was pretty, and that people liked to look at me as if I were a flower. His smile persisted, and I noticed one of his front teeth was missing.

"Good morning," I said hesitatingly. Whenever meeting someone new, I shrink inside. What if they look too closely and see the real me? That terrible thing I did. Maybe the way I behaved, or talked, or looked at another person would give it away. I was always self-conscious, trying to find the right words, a gesture, an expression to hide who I really was. It was tiring to be someone else all the time, but it got easier. "I'm here to apply for the barista job. I saw the ad in the newspaper."

He measured me up and down, an unusual way to test someone's abilities, and then he spoke. "Okay. Have you ever worked as a barista?"

"No." I said. "But I'm willing to learn."

"Excellent. When can you start?" Everything in my life until then had been difficult, apparently except for getting a job in L.A.

"Whenever." I shrugged.

"Tomorrow?"

"Sure." I smiled.

He extended his hand and said, "You're hired." We shook on it. He continued. "Your pay is sixteen dollars per hour. You'll do morning shifts one week, and afternoon shifts the next. Then rotate. My name's Brian and I'm the owner of this place. I'm here if you have questions." He paused for a second as if I had something to say, but I didn't. "And one more thing. You get a free cup of coffee every day. Your boyfriend gets a discount."

"My boyfriend?" I said.

"Yes. Your boyfriend. You have a boyfriend?"

"No."

He smiled. "Well, that makes it easier, doesn't it? No discount needed."

"Right," I said.

"Oh, and one more thing." He lifted his index finger and pointed in my direction. "Don't be late. Ever. I need you here fifteen minutes early. If you can't make it early, then at least come on time."

I nodded. I looked around to familiarize myself with

the space, then gazed back at Brian and asked, "So, what makes this café popular?"

"What?" He grimaced.

"The ad says the café is popular in L.A. What's so popular about it?"

"Lots of history here." He grinned. "Lots of friendships made. That's just our signature."

CHAPTER TEN

The following night passed without gunshots. As I found my bearings in the morning, I looked out the window and saw another sunny day. It was my first day at a new workplace. As I lay on the futon, I rubbed my eyes and muttered something under my breath. The upstairs neighbor was stomping in his apartment. I grabbed my phone from the floor and opened it up to check my email. The apartment didn't have Wi-Fi, nor was I going to get it, because it was too expensive. It was enough to pay an exuberant amount for the unlimited data plan on my phone.

I swiped my email and noticed one from my mother.

Subject: I miss you

Hi honey,

How's L.A.? It's been only a couple of days since you left home, but I already miss you. Let me know if there's anything you need from me.

Kisses and hugs,
Mom

I shook my head. Maybe I'd respond to her later.

I stood up and looked at my facial expression in the mirror. I did it often when I practiced acting. My eyes narrowed as I concentrated on my posture. It looked good.

"Are you talkin' to me?" Slight pause. "Are you talkin' to me?"

I turned around as if I was looking for someone and turned back to look in the mirror. "Then who else are you talkin' to? Are you talking to me?"

The first time I impersonated the young Robert De Niro, my mom laughed hard, followed up with a high praise, "Oh my goodness, Sam, you are a natural. You have a special gift. You sound just like him."

Robert De Niro was my idol. Next to him, Meryl Streep was another favorite. When I watched their movies, I'd be glued to the screen and not blink, absorbing their moves, studying the intonation of their voices, watching every single gesture.

My first encounter with stage performing, besides my own, happened when I turned sixteen. Mother had periods of being drug-clean. At those times, she was far more generous and loving towards me. She attempted to make me happy. The year I turned sixteen, Mother took out some of her savings and gifted me a trip to New York City. As soon as we found our hotel and entered our room, Mom pulled two tickets for a Broadway show out of her purse.

I thought maybe Mom got us tickets to a cool play like

Mamma Mia or Chicago, but they ended up being for
Medea. I found out years later that Mom couldn't get us to
see any other play, because all the others were too expensive. A more terrifying occurrence was the play itself when
Medea killed all of her children on the stage to avenge her
husband, Jason. When Medea killed her last child, I saw
my mother shifting in her seat back and forth, avoiding
eyes with me even though I landed mine on hers,
wondering if she took me to this one on purpose. She later
apologized while crying, and I told her it was okay; she
couldn't have known what the play was about.

I snapped out of my thoughts and got ready for work.
Brian told me I had to be there by eight at the latest. If I
were an expert judge of character, and I felt I was, Brian
seemed sketchy. His strange, alluring look made me
nervous, and I wondered what was lingering in his mind
when he first met me. But there was no time to think. I
smiled in relief that I at least had a job.

CHAPTER ELEVEN

I arrived at Spy Café around eight, and Brian showed me where everything was located: the porcelain coffee mugs were for customers staying at the cafe while paper cups were meant for coffee to go. The coffee shop had only two tables, and at each table were three chairs. The atmosphere was far from pleasant, and I couldn't picture anyone staying longer than minutes. He explained how the coffee machine worked and where the decaf one was kept warm. His words were slow and drawn out as if he was explaining to a five-year-old. I had been a coffee drinker since I was ten, and I knew a little about it. Explaining this to him would be fruitless, so I'd stepped aside when he showed me how to do things and listened. None of it was difficult, but he wanted to ensure I made no mistakes when customers arrived. He wanted to cut the wait time from five minutes to two, when possible, hoping his happy customers would return.

The minute I started working on the coffee machine, he watched my every step. He'd click his tongue when I did something he wouldn't approve of. "Nope, that's not how it goes."

He reminded me of my father when, during his worst time of fatherhood, became critical of everything my mother and I did. Whenever a small action of ours annoyed him, he'd yell at us and give us mean looks. Over time, my body felt charged with fear and anxiety in Father's presence. I did nothing intentionally to anger him, but I also didn't know what would set him off next, so I stayed away from him as much as possible. My room was my favorite place to be. I tuned out and ignored Brian's constant yapping until he made his voice more pleasant and said, "Sam, we're opening the doors in fifteen minutes. Be ready and smile. You don't smile enough, you know. It won't cost you a thing."

I said nothing, but what I wanted to tell him he was no exception to that. I swear, this guy never smiled in his life.

"Sure, Brian. I'll do my best."

As I was moving the clean mugs from the dishwasher to the shelves below the cash register, the door opened and a man walked in. He waved at me and gave me a quick smile. Before I had a chance to ask him what he wanted, he continued walking until he arrived behind the counter where I stood. He extended his hand to shake mine and said, "I'm Michael. You must be Sam."

Michael turned out to be my coworker, a little older than me. He was plump, and he needed a haircut. His hair was sweaty from the LA heat, and it looked like a helmet on his enormous head.

Michael was a chatty fellow. He'd tell me crazy stories about their customers. Like, one time when a woman came in and ordered a double expresso. Michael told her that the coffee was actually called espresso, but she argued it was expresso, because it was made at a rapid service, hence express. Or, another time, a young lad came in and once he ordered his coffee, he took a jar of pennies from his backpack and handed it to Michael. He had a funny way of telling his stories; I could see him performing stand-up comedy.

I liked Michael—he seemed good-natured and a nice guy.

Several times during our shift, I caught Michael looking at me. When our eyes locked, he'd wink at me, smile, and turn around. When I served a customer, Michael was on his phone, texting with his thumbs with a speed of light. I wondered who he was texting so much. When the customer left, he'd shift his attention back to me and add, "Hey."

Brian came out of his office once in a while, hands resting on his waist, watching us. Neither one paid any attention to Brian as we focused on the task at hand. The cafe wasn't busy in the slightest, and Michael had plenty of time to tell me his stories, which broke up an otherwise monotonous morning. This job wasn't ideal, but it would do it while I auditioned and settled on my acting.

At the end of my shift on my first day at the cafe, I was standing at the counter, and I felt Michael's body close to mine. He was standing behind me. "Hey, Sam. There's a cool new restaurant that I'd like to check out. Would you... would you like to come with me?"

Fear washed over me. My heart raced as I pondered Michael's question. My biggest fear, in any new situation, was getting closer to anyone who might try to dig into my dirty past. I started moving the mugs from the upper shelf to the lower shelf so I would appear to be busy. My eyes diverted from Michael's direction, avoiding his like a plague.

"I don't know, Michael. I don't have money for extravagant dinners, you know."

"Oh, I know. Look where we work." He laughed. I gave him an inquisitive look. What was that supposed to mean? But Michael jumped in to clarify. "I mean, minimum wage?" He looked at me like a puppy and shrugged his shoulders.

"Right." I said.

"I work a second job as a freelance writer, and I could afford to buy dinner for both of us. What do you say?"

He smiled when I looked at him again.

"I don't know, Michael. As a rule of thumb, I don't date co-workers. It'd be just too weird."

"I get it, but..."

I stood up from my kneeling position and looked at Michael. My body faced his and we could no longer avoid eye contact. As I examined his out of shape body, I realized Michael wasn't my type. A hint of boldness came over me and I said, "Michael, I'm just not in a better place in life to date right now. Sorry. Let's be friends, okay?"

Michael didn't flinch or have any type of reaction. He only said, "Okay."

As I was ready to leave for the day, I looked at Michael to say goodbye. He stood at the counter, hands resting in his pockets, giving me a sinister look. Perhaps he hadn't taken my words so well after all. I opened the door and walked away as fast as humanly possible.

CHAPTER TWELVE

The following day, I showed up at the cafe, and Michael had already started his shift. He smiled at me when I entered and said his usual, "Hey." I felt relieved that he no longer seemed upset. I didn't intend to make him angry with my rejection. It was just that my sense of self-preservation was stronger than any attempt to get close to another human.

My second day of work was pretty much the same as the previous shift had been. Michael would still ogle me and give me an occasional wink, and I'd do my best to dodge it. Brian still watched me from around the corner and stormed out to give me instructions when I seemingly messed up.

Back home, I'd had a rosier idea of what my life in L.A. would become. Working in a dingy cafe wasn't it. Things in my mind had seemed a lot brighter before I ventured on this journey. It's funny how our mind conjures thoughts we accept as reality. Our thoughts become our truth that we carry like an amulet. The same way I carried the truth about my parents: they were bad people, even though my mother thought going to church made her feel superior.

Escaping from home and my mother needed to happen. I didn't think I'd face challenges that were just as bad here, if not worse. I'd pictured a life that would burst at seams with opportunities, and I'd be grabbing them like candy after busting a pinata. But this was no party. I felt lost, and I didn't know where to begin. All I knew was that I couldn't lose sight of my acting dream, no matter how difficult it would be to achieve. I looked forward to the day I resigned from this job, but I had no other options yet. A young woman from a small town didn't have too many choices. I was scrambling to figure out how to audition for acting gigs; it couldn't be that difficult, but I had to be competing against thousands of other eager and talented actors.

Michael's voice stopped my thoughts from running wild. He kept saying my name while I stared at the coffee machine as if it could transport me to a different place. If only.

"Sam!" He raised his voice. That got my attention. "Sorry about that." He apologized to our customer.

I turned around and there stood a man staring right at me. His eyes were penetrating, and he wore a smile. He didn't seem to be upset by the wait.

"Oh." I said. "What would you like?"

"I'll have a latte." He said. "Actually, no. Make that an espresso."

He knew not to say expresso, and that put a smile on my face.

"Coming right up," I announced.

I walked up to the espresso machine and while I

worked on it; I felt his eyes on my back. On my left, Brian stood near the door of his office and nodded at me. His lips parted into a big, toothless smile, but his eyes were wicked. I wondered why this creep would nod at me like that.

I turned around and noticed our customer still resting his eyes on me. Michael was standing at the cash register, counting the coins and sorting them in the register bins. He tried to look busy, as if boredom was a sin.

The man kept smiling and said, "It's hot today."

"Don't even get me started." I snorted. I put my head down to divert my eyes from him, and when I looked up, I noticed him staring at my cleavage. I had unbuttoned my tee earlier because of the heat and had forgotten to button it up. I raised my voice to get his attention away from it. "That will be three dollars and fifteen cents."

The man looked at me while trying to locate his wallet in his shorts' pockets. "Darn it. I think I left my wallet in my car."

While he was reaching for his other pockets, tapping his body with his hands, I noticed how beautifully sculpted he was. Great muscles. A perfect body. A smile to die for. His straight, white teeth were blinding me and his smile soothed me.

"Oh, wait." He reached for his back pocket and pulled out his wallet. "I knew I took it with me."

A sigh of relief came out of me. Last thing I wanted was for my shift to end paying some stranger's coffee. He handed me five dollars and told me to keep the change.

"I don't think I've seen you here before," he said.

"I'm new." I cut it short. My shift was supposed to end at three, but Vanessa, the girl who was supposed to replace me, was running late. Again. She always blamed it on the poor transportation system in L.A. She was right—public transportation in L.A. needed help, but she could plan accordingly.

Michael stood next to me and listened in to our conversation.

"So, what's the young lady doing in LA?" he asked.

I tilted my head to examine his intentions, but his continuous smile gave nothing away. After a brief silence, I said, "Whatever most people do here in L.A."

He laughed. "And what is that?"

"I moved to L.A. to give myself a shot at acting."

"Ah, of course," he said. "And how's it going so far?"

I put my head down, thinking of Stacey, and shook my head. I clenched my fist and mustered the words out, "Not as I expected." A smile formed on my face to hide the pain.

"Those things take time, you know." He kept smiling at me as if he knew my experience had been nothing but disappointing. "I have several friends in the industry. I'd be more than happy to connect them with you."

I tried hard to subdue my excitement. "You do?"

He nodded. "Yep. If anything, they can give you a few tips or connect you with others who could help."

"Sure." I said. It sounded too good to be true. It felt like I had just won the lottery after being so desperate for an excellent opportunity. This might be it.

"If you want to give me your phone number or email address, I'd be happy to forward it to my friends."

I searched for a piece of paper and a pen around me, but he handed me his phone and said, "Here, just enter it on my phone."

I grabbed his phone and jotted down my phone number. When I gave him the phone back, he looked down and said, "Sam? Oh, what a beautiful name."

He paid and left the café, leaving me with a smile on my face. I watched him stop in front of his BMW, staring at his phone. Then he turned around, waved at me, and entered his car. I felt a vibration in my pocket and took my phone out. A message from an unknown sender.

It was nice to meet you, Sam. You are lovely. Hope to see you soon. Corey

I opened up the message, and in the corner, I clicked on Save Entry. Corey was now permanently stored in my phone address book. I wouldn't let him get away.

CHAPTER THIRTEEN

After my shift, I stopped by a grocery store in order to half-fill the fridge. My eating habits changed after Father died. Some people find comfort in food when they deal with something heavy in life, but not me. My mother gained several pounds when she became a widow and since then she'd never stopped complaining about her big thighs and double chin. Food made me nauseous. I saw it as a mere necessity for survival. My shopping cart comprised a loaf of bread, popcorn, mayonnaise, two avocados, and bologna. I always thought of Judge Judy every time I encountered bologna.

I came home, dragging my feet up the stairs. The L.A. heat made me sluggish. The building elevator still wasn't working. I entered the apartment and turned the TV on as soon as I crossed the threshold. The TV had only a few channels—no cable—but one of them ran movies all day long.

I made myself a bologna sandwich and popcorn, and sat down on the futon to watch a movie. My phone rang.

It was my mother. I rolled my eyes, contemplating whether to answer. Talking to her on the phone was never an uplifting experience. If I could avoid it, I would by all means.

"Hi, Mom." My voice was a mix of joy and boredom.

"Hi, darling. How are you? I miss you." She sounded like she was crying.

"I miss you, too, Mom." But I didn't miss her at all.

"When are you coming to visit?"

"Mom, I just moved here."

"Oh, I know, baby. But it's felt like years." An awkward silence arrived. I took the remote in my hand and paused the movie. What's Eating Gilbert Grape. One of my all-time favorites. "Sam?" My mom called me as if she'd lost me.

"Yes, Mom. I'm still here."

"How about if I came to visit you? Maybe next month?"

I looked around my place and pictured my mother sleeping on the floor in a corner of this dump. She probably wouldn't care as long as we were together, but a feeling of caution nagged at me. If she came to visit, the image of this dungeon would stay in her head and, knowing my mom, she'd feel sorry for me. I wanted to avoid her pity at all costs.

"I've been busy these days with auditioning and stuff. I don't think we'd be spending much time together, anyway." My auditioning efforts had been fruitless so far. I'd applied for a dozen auditions, but my applications seemed to disappear into the black hole.

"Oh." I sensed disappointment in her voice. "I understand, darling. It's good to hear you've been auditioning, though. That's what you're there for, right?"

I removed the popcorn shell from between my teeth and looked at my finger to see the offender. These little stinkers. It struck me as sad that the popcorn shell was getting more of my attention than my mother was.

"Right," I responded, indifferent. "Listen, Mom. As soon as I get my act together—and no pun intended—I'll come home. Promise."

"You promise?"

"Yes. In the meantime, I want you to stop worrying. Okay? It's not helping either of us."

My mother sighed, and her breath sounded like a belligerent wind.

"I know, sweetheart. I'm sorry. I'm really trying. This is our first time being apart." That wasn't true. When she went away to a rehab, she didn't see herself as leaving me behind, and I was just a child then.

"I gotta go. All's fine. You take care of yourself."

The phone went dead.

As soon as we hung up, I saw a text message on my phone. It was from Corey. An immediate smile formed on my face.

Hey Sam. And FYI—one of my friends in the acting industry will get in touch with you soon. His name is Chris. Talk soon!

I took a popcorn and put it in my mouth. I reread his message a million times over until it sunk in. My dream would finally come true. I would be an actress soon.

The afternoon turned into a night. I had been watching movies all afternoon, without realizing that the time slipped away. My apartment would have been pitch black had it not been for the lights projecting from the TV. Outside, commotion ensued. People were roaring like wild animals. They were having a shouting match, spitting out the f-bombs. In a distance, the cop cars sent a wave of the sirens. What was happening? I crawled down on my knees and came up to the window. It was ajar, and I moved it by inches in slow motion, not to draw attention to myself.

A hint of fear trickled down my spine. Down below on the street, a number of men had got into a fistfight. About five hundred feet away, a man hurried along the sidewalk, speeding up with each step. Everything looked so close, as if I were watching a violent movie from my close-up TV screen. The action below was orchestrated perfectly, making it suspenseful. The man who approached raised his right arm, and to my shock, shot from a pistol he was holding in his hand.

Bang.

To avoid screaming, I covered my mouth with my hand and dropped to the floor for cover. My hands shook. My heart was pounding in my neck. The outside screams amplified; someone asking for help. The sounds soon got replaced by the police sirens. I sat on the floor for a while, unable to move. I had never been exposed to such blatant violence. For the first time, I feared for my life, and I realized then how much I didn't want to lose it.

CHAPTER FOURTEEN

Shaken by the previous night, I walked along the street charged with fear as I made my way to work. I could not unsee the man with a gun, moving forward and shooting at someone. Whenever I thought about death, those pictures kept forcing themselves inside my mind. Images of my father, the blood draining from his lifeless body. Were some lives more valuable than others? Was my father, a man with violent tendencies, worthier than my mom, a devoted church goer? If all of us disappeared into oblivion in the end, what moral compass was needed to justify a death of another? These thoughts haunted me for years. I'd spent enough time alone for them to be conjured in seconds and before lingering inside me for longer than I could handle. To this day, I still hadn't solved the puzzle.

I got through my next shift, and then my next, and continued to apply for auditions, giving life its chance to reach its full potential. Meeting Corey had given me a hint of hope, especially after he'd shared that his friend Chris was going to contact me soon.

A few days passed, and Chris still hadn't contacted me. Michelle would advise me to be patient, but my patience was wearing off. I was checking my phone as often as I could. When I saw that someone other than Chris texted me, I'd tuck my phone back in my pocket, ignoring the message and falling deeper into despair.

On day four, when I was still waiting for Chris to message me, Corey showed up at Spy Café, wearing his usual smile. When he walked in, it felt like a ray of sunshine brightened the space. Michael, who stood next to me, looked at Corey with panicky eyes and disappeared into the corner as soon as Corey greeted us. What was that all about? Perhaps he was feeling intimated next to a handsome guy who took the liking to me. Vanessa would probably appreciate Corey more, but so far, both of his visits occurred when I was working with Michael.

"Hi, Corey." I said. "Nice to see you."

"Nice seeing you as well." Corey said. "I was in the neighborhood and thought I'd stop by."

"That's great. It's always good to see you." No other customer captivated me like Corey did. Maybe it had something to do with his promise to take off my acting career. The way he looked at me and spoke to me made me believe in myself. And he obviously thought I showed promise if he was willing to share his contacts with me. His visits made my shifts at Spy Café more bearable, something to look forward to.

"It's always good to be seen." He smiled.

"Hey, thanks for giving Chris my phone number. I hope to hear from him soon."

"Oh." His face changed into a grimace like he didn't want this topic to be brought up. "Yeah... that. Chris travels a lot, so I wouldn't be surprised if you have to wait a little longer."

"Sure, no problem." Inside, it felt like a punch in the gut.

Another customer walked in and immediately drew her eyes to the menu board behind me. She was wearing headphones and music could be heard through them. I looked around to see where Michael was to help her, but he was nowhere to be found. The woman seemed to be in her own world and didn't mind the waiting.

"Hey, listen, Sam." Corey looked at me with puppy eyes and suddenly blushing, he said, "Would you be interested in going out for a coffee, or maybe a walk?"

I liked his subtle way of asking me out.

I nodded. "Um, yeah, sure. Why not?"

"Great! I'll text you soon to decide on a time and location."

He looked down at his phone and quickly typed a message. While looking down, he said, "Sorry, I just need to send a quick text to my friend. He can be so needy." He looked up and laughed, then turned back to his phone.

Just as he finished, Michael walked in. He looked serious. His shoulders were slumped forward, and he had a depressed look in his eyes. I wondered what was happening in his life as of late. He told me he couldn't come to work the other day because something came up. I was glad that he wasn't present when Corey asked me out on a date. Why put more salt on the open wound?.

That whole day, I giggled and greeted our customers in a cheerful voice. Brian came out one time and stared at me with eyes wide open. He shook his head and returned to his office, where he spent most of his time. Now I had to wait for another person to contact me. But this one I was more excited about.

CHAPTER FIFTEEN

Corey didn't wait long. He texted me the following day, asking if I was free that evening. It was Friday, and I'd come home from work at four o'clock, with nothing better to do. The walls of my apartment had a strange effect on me; I expected a gruesome fight outside any minute, and being there made me feel uneasy. Corey's text cheered me up. The second it arrived, I forgot all about the neighborhood dangers that surrounded me.

I was sitting on my futon, watching Ocean's 11, the movie I had seen many times. The lines were too familiar, and I'd memorized most of them. I didn't want to appear too eager, so I waited to respond to Corey. I stood up and walked to the kitchen sink to pour myself a glass of water. The water tasted like iron and I poured it out of the glass and left it on the countertop. I opened up the fridge, stared at it for a minute, not thinking about what I was looking at. I slammed the fridge closed and walked back to the futon, hoisting myself on top. My hands were shaking.

I took my phone and typed back the message to Corey. Yes.

The three dots showing typing appeared and his text came through.

Great. Pick you up at six. What's your address?

I sent him my address and at the moment wondered if he realized how dangerous my neighborhood was. Not that it mattered much. I jumped off the couch and walked to my luggage, where I still stored all my clothes. The apartment didn't have any closets, so I figured I'd leave my clothes in one place. I rummaged through the bag, looking for the best outfit I could find for the occasion. A red short dress fit me well and I placed it on the bed to air it out. I spent the next hour pampering myself. After taking a hot bath, I took time to perfect my make-up. I was pleased with my appearance, and I hoped Corey would be, too.

The red dress looked perfect on me. I looked like I just came from of a Hollywood red-carpet event. Corey better tell Chris he wouldn't regret meeting with me, investing in me. I was born to be an actress.

My tummy growled, signaling hunger. I'd eaten little all day. I went to the bathroom and sprayed perfume on my neck and my left wrist. As I rubbed my wrists together, the sweet aroma dazzled my senses. For a second, it made me dizzy, so I closed my eyes to compose myself.

It had been a while since I'd been on a date. My one and only serious, short-term boyfriend back home broke up with me when he left town for college in Massachusetts. He and I weren't a good couple. He was an odd duck, with the unusual dream to finish college, unmatched to most people of our age in Gallup. We'd spent time going to museums, bookshops, and playing games at the arcade, which I'd thrown myself into even though none of these activities interested me much. To my disappointment, he just ended our relationship, cutting out any chance of us building a future together or making plans to meet while he studied.

"Sam." Erik had looked at me with a sense of seriousness and pride. "I don't think a long-distance relationship will work for me. Four years is a long time, and I'll be busy with school, anyway. Sorry. I like you, but I'm too young to get tied to one person. Things will work themselves out, I'm sure."

I cried and gave him a hug. His limp arms enveloped me, then pushed me away.

"One more thing. Go live your life. Follow your dreams. Forget boyfriends. Good ones will come when they're destined to." He smiled and gave me a tighter hug.

At six o'clock, I shuffled down the stairs of my building, holding onto the rail. My black stilettos felt wobbly under my feet, but they complemented my red dress. When I stepped outside, Corey had parked his BMW in front of the building. He was staring down at what I reasoned was his phone. My silhouette startled him, but his mouth dropped when he saw my transformation from a sweaty, disheveled barista to a spruced-up woman.

He jumped out of the car and walked in my direction. "Sam, oh my goodness. You look gorgeous."

He looked me up and down, then gave me a big, long hug. I smiled, pleased at his delight.

"And you smell nice, too. Let's go."

He led me to the passenger side of the car and opened the door for me. What a perfect gentleman. He sat down at the wheel and I looked at him inquisitively. "Where are you taking me?"

"I made a reservation at a restaurant. I'm sure you're going to love. It is just outside of L.A., close to my house. It's my favorite place."

"Oh, perfect." My stomach kept growling. I took a glance at Corey, and he looked incredible. My heart skipped a beat at the thought of sitting opposite him in a restaurant. I couldn't wait to see what the night had in store.

CHAPTER SIXTEEN

As soon as we arrived at the restaurant, the hostess greeted Corey as if they were best friends. They awkwardly high-fived, then hugged. Asking no questions, she grabbed a couple of menus and brought us to a table next to a window. Outside, a breathtaking view of the Temescal Gateway Park stretched for miles away. The crescent moon shone high in the sky, giving away the youth of the evening. But the outside view didn't quite match Corey's dashing looks.

He was clean shaven, and he wore a casual shirt with slacks and fancy shoes. A golden chain protruded from the scruff of his neck, decorating his handsome features. This was the first time I could look at Corey up close and in person. It was like I'd just taken Mona Lisa down from the wall and studied each brush stroke in more detail.

"You look great," I said.

"Thanks. I had to look good for this special occasion." He smiled. His cheek dimple looked like a little jewel on a crown. "I'm curious, Sam. Why do you want to become an actress?"

I shrugged at first, like it was a question with an obvious answer. But part of me knew Corey was taking an interest in me and wanted to know more. Peeling the onion layers.

"When I was little, I watched movies a lot, and I impersonated the actors. It was fun to do that, but more so, I enjoyed being somebody else for the time being."

He furrowed his brows and tilted his head. "Why is that? You don't like yourself?"

As he asked that question, I was relieved that our waitress came to our table and asked what we wanted to drink. Our plump waitress, with hair long to her waist, blushed while gazing at Corey. She fluttered her eyelashes and diverted her eyes as she took our order.

Corey studied the wine menu and looked at me. I told him I didn't drink alcohol.

He raised his brows and said, "Oh." He took the wine menu and handed it back to the waitress. "I will stick with water then. And the lady can order whatever she wants."

"I'll have a diet Coke."

As soon as the waiter left, Corey looked at me and smiled. He'd clearly forgotten he'd asked me about not liking myself. The knowledge I didn't drink alcohol seemed to have set a different mood.

"I think it's really cool that you don't drink. And that you want to become an actress. Both are quite admirable." I felt like I was earning brownie points. "Let me see you act a little."

I looked around to see if anyone was watching. Sometimes, I'd feel embarrassed about these things. I didn't want to be a novelty act, seeking attention. But no one in our proximity bothered to look at us.

I made an upside "U" with my mouth and with a raspy voice and an Italian accent, I began impersonating Don Corleone. "That I cannot do." I scratched a corner of my mouth with a pinky and continued. The whole monologue flew out of my mouth while Corey watched me with eyes wide open. He seemed amused.

When I finished, I changed my face expression to normal and smiled at Corey. He burst out laughing, and said, "Don Corleone, Don Corleone! That's perfect, Sam! You're so talented. I can't wait to tell Chris all about you."

My eyes widened. "You will? What are you planning on telling him?"

He studied my eyes for a short while longer and said. "You're not just talented, Sam. You're more than that. I like you. I really do. You seem very special. I think you deserve all the success in the world."

"I do?"

He nodded. "I have good instincts about people. They are razor sharp. I can tell right away who's an asshole and who is a decent human being. You seem like a decent person."

A lump formed in my throat. Corey wouldn't know what I did as a child, and I hoped he never would. The waitress stopped by to set a glass of soda in front of me, and I grabbed it as soon as she placed it on the table.

I felt my cheeks redden from his remarks and the heat built up in my body. Besides Michelle and my mother, who tried hard to butter me up, no one else ever gave me compliments. I was so unaccustomed to it that Corey's compliments sounded to me as if he was praising a statue.

But I had to ground myself and learn more about Corey. I didn't know what he did for work or how he was spending his leisure time besides stopping by Spy Café to buy his coffee. Why was he bothered about helping me? I didn't understand. But I'd be a fool not to take him up on it. This was my only opportunity to get closer to my dream.

"So, what do you do, Corey?"

He sipped water from his glass and placed it down on the table as if he was getting ready to give an entire speech.

"I'm a pilot."

"A pilot? What planes do you fly?"

He looked up and frowned as if thinking of an answer, then added, "Let's see. I mostly fly commercial planes, but every once in a while, an executive will hire me to fly their private jet."

He looked at me and smiled.

"How long have you been doing that?"

"For about fifteen years. I started quite young."

"Sounds like you really love what you do."

"That I do." He paused and looked at me. "Perhaps I will give you a ride above L.A. one of these days. What say you?"

"That would be amazing." Corey was amazing. "I always wanted to see the city from a bird's eye view."

"Deal." Corey said.

CHAPTER SEVENTEEN

Once dinner had been wrapped up, Corey grabbed my hand and led me to his car before opening the passenger door. I entered the car gingerly and looked ahead. The night had turned dark, and the stars were twinkling like diamonds. I didn't want the glory of this night to end. Just as I was daring to hope that I could hang out with Corey a little longer, he said, "Sam, I hope I'm not being too presumptuous, but... would you like to come by my house tonight and maybe watch a movie?"

I trembled with excitement, but I worked hard at concealing it. "Well, I need to go to work tomorrow morning, so I can't stay up too late." I didn't want to sound desperate.

"No worries. I'll get you home before ten." He gazed at me for a second and smiled.

Corey said his house wasn't too far from the restaurant. He drove off the road and onto a private long path surrounded by vegetation. It was very dark outside, and if it wasn't for the high beams, we could see nothing in front of our finger. Corey drove fast and looked ahead, his eyes trained on the road. I gave him an occasional look, studying his serious face, and admired his manly features.

Corey stopped in front of a long, metal gate enveloped by arborvitae on each side. The lights emanating from the house in front of us gave it a sense of life. Along the fence were the high and thick hedges, hiding everything behind them. Beyond the gate stood a water fountain, a carefully cut lawn and bushes that surrounded the enormous house. I was used to houses this big, but not as luxurious as this one. The house my grandparents had bought in Yah-ta-hey was huge next to the other houses in the vicinity.

I had only seen houses like the one in front of me in fancy magazines and movies. This one reminded me of mansions in Newport, Rhode Island, that I'd seen in pictures. Majestic, grand, and beautiful.

Corey pushed a button in the car, and the gate opened. He pulled in and parked on the cul-de-sac in front of the house. I finally got the words out of my mouth. "Wow, you live here?"

He laughed. "Indeed."

When we exited the car, I saw a swimming pool on the side of the house and a tennis court close to it. A strange desire pulled at me to run on the grass; to spin and jump around like a Yoyo and embrace it all. But Corey's voice brought me back to reality. "Are you coming in?"

As I stepped inside, the beautiful dream continued. The house featured a spiral staircase leading to the second floor, a large and crystal chandelier hanging from the ceiling. The high ceilings gave an enormity to the place alongside the decor and the expensive paintings on the walls. Vases with fresh flowers were everywhere, and large delicate marble statues were perched in many corners of the house, making the place look like a museum. I didn't know what to check out first; everything was just as perfect as Corey was.

We stood in the center of the large foyer, and Corey extended both arms. Pointing in each direction, he said, "Right wing. Left wing."

"Wow," I said. "Your house has wings? I hope it doesn't fly away."

He laughed. "That's funny."

He took my hand and led me to the guest room; one of the many rooms in the house.

"Make yourself comfortable. Want something to drink? Juice, soda, water?"

"Water is fine." He walked to the kitchen and turned on the sink to pour water into two glasses. I heard him from the guest room, opening the cabinet and rumbling around. He returned with two glasses of water, smiling. "Here you go." He placed them on the coaster on the table and sat next to me.

Heat emanated heat from his body as he sat next to me. His cologne smelled sweet and inviting. "So? What movie do you want to watch?"

"Ummm." I was giving it some thought, ill-prepared for the question. "How about Kramer versus Kramer?"

"Kramer versus Kramer? The old movie with Dustin Hoffman and Meryl Streep?"

"Yep, that's the one." I expected him to know the movie, since it had been around for a long time.

He turned the TV on and searched through the vast number of movie titles. When he finally found the one, he clicked on play and it began.

I couldn't concentrate on the movie. Corey's presence distracted me too much. It had been a while since I'd sat down with another human being to watch a movie. Michelle didn't enjoy watching movies, because she couldn't rest in one place for more than half an hour. She'd quit within fifteen minutes.

Corey's eyes focused on the movie as he relaxed on the couch. His left arm was touching my right arm while his right arm was dangling along the couch.

As the movie progressed, I felt the heat of his body nearing me until he wrapped his arm around my neck. He kissed my temple, which made me smile.

When the child came on the screen, Corey turned to me and whispered, "Sam, do you want to have children?"

When I was a teenager, my mother had attempted to teach me about relationships and intimacy, even though she was far from being qualified. Once, she'd told me that when a man was serious about a relationship, he would inquire about a woman's wants and needs in her life. The man would ask whether the woman wanted to have children, signaling his seriousness about her. My mom added something about testing the waters and finding out if your date was a perfect match.

I blushed at this question as the words my mother once spoke washed over me.

"Well," I began. "Eventually. I'm still trying to get my career going."

Corey nodded. "That's admirable." He smiled at me, keeping his gaze long and fixated on me. "What would you want to have? A boy or a girl?"

I laughed. That question never crossed my mind

before. I was barely trying to survive, never mind thinking of my imaginary child's gender.

"It doesn't really matter," I said. "As long as the baby is healthy and alive."

"Good answer." Corey leaned forward and picked up his water glass, gulping it all at once. He put the glass back on the table and grabbed mine. He turned around and asked, "You want some?"

"Sure." I drank my water and handed the glass to him. He put it down on the table and leaned back on the couch, moving away from me. Time swirled around and I could no longer tell where I was or what I was doing. My body stopped belonging to me and it was as if I'd lost all of my senses. My eyes felt heavy and the lids involuntarily closed. The TV screen blurred, and then everything else went dark.

CHAPTER EIGHTEEN

I woke up in the morning in a room with high ceilings. Panic came over me when I realized I wasn't lying on my futon. Where was I? Under me was a king-size bed with satin covers that smelled of lavender. I had never felt such comfort and softness while sleeping before. The room seemed enormous, with long bay windows on the side overlooking the front yard. Fresh sunrays gently filtered in and reached the edge of my bed. It was like being on an open field overlooking the universe. On the opposite side of the bed sat a dresser with a long mirror. I saw my head in the mirror peeking from behind the cover. I rubbed my eyes to see if I'd been dreaming. Perhaps I'd died and was waking up in the afterlife.

A note on the pillow next to me drew my attention. I picked it up, and the first word in the note was something that I was most familiar with: my name. I rolled to my side and placed my right elbow on the bed while I read the note.

· · ·

Sam, you fell asleep fast, and I didn't want to wake you up. Hope you had a good night's sleep. I'm sorry I had to leave so early in the morning. One of my clients needed a ride to Las Vegas. You know those gambling types! Haha. Talk soon. Corey

P.S. to get out of the house, the gate's code is 1115.

Corey's note put a smile on my face. He was thoughtful and kind. The fear and confusion I had felt began to recede, although I couldn't help feeling worried that I couldn't recall anything much from the previous night after watching the movie. Corey must have carried me to this room, and I couldn't even remember him picking me up. I must have fallen asleep during the movie. It was one I'd seen many times, and maybe my eyes couldn't fight to stay awake. The comfort of being near Corey perhaps lulled me to sleep. How could I have gotten into such a deep sleep that nothing fazed me? I had gotten little sleep the night before, and I'd not eaten much during the day before our meal, so it was possible I was tired and the food coma got me.

I stood from the bed, feeling rested and ready to start my day. The wall clock in the hallway showed it was past eight o'clock, and I quickened my steps through the house in panic. I should have been at work by now. Brian was going to kill me, but I would try to come up with an excuse on my way there.

I opened up my phone and searched through the apps like a lunatic. Once I located the Uber app, I called a car, which told me it was five minutes away. Relieved, I walked outside the house and headed toward the gate. I entered the code Corey left, and the gate moved in my direction. I exited through the gate, and it moved until it shut. Instinctively, I grabbed the bars and shook them, as if trying to escape, but the gate was locked.

While waiting for my ride to arrive, I looked around the property. Its size stunned me over again. It looked even more impressive in the daylight. I whispered to myself, "Wow."

My ride arrived, and I turned around to look at the house one more time. Part of me hoped this would not be the first and last time I entered it. I could see myself swimming in the pool and basking in the sun, or playing tennis with Corey. But if I was going to get fired from my job for being so late, being in the nicest place on Earth barely mattered. I'd be screwed without my only source of income.

I jumped in the car and noticed the driver staring at the house. He didn't even greet me. He asked, "You live here?"

I scoffed, "I wish." If he had known that the place he was taking me was my workplace where Brian paid me minimum wage, he wouldn't have bothered to ask me this question.

As I was leaving this giant property basked in all its glory, an uneasy feeling nudged me: why was Corey, a good-looking and rich person, still single? And why did he need to live in a house this big?

Many rich people liked to boast about their wealth and buy enormous houses, even if they barely used them. I'd possibly do the same if I could. A house like Corey's would beat my little studio apartment with the noisy bass player above it.

As for still being single, I had no explanation. Was I so

lucky to have met him and hit it off like this? Maybe he'd been in many relationships before, but I'd heard rumors that L.A. women were self-centered and spoiled, and perhaps that didn't suit Corey. Who knew? All I knew was that I couldn't wait to tell Michelle about Corey. She'd squeal in excitement for me.

The ride to Spy Café took about thirty minutes. Even though the rush hour had died down a bit, some stretches of it persisted. I could only imagine what Brian would say to me when I walked through the door. When Brian hired me, he'd warned me about being late. Would he really fire me? I would tell him an accident caused the traffic to stop, and we stood in one place for over twenty minutes and didn't move until the cars cleared. And that was easy to believe since it was such a usual occurrence in L.A. I needed to stay calm in case he asked more questions and needed more convincing.

As soon as I walked in, Michael whistled when he saw me wearing my red dress.

"Oh, stop it." I waved my hand and smiled.

"Coming from a hot date?"

I blushed. Of course, I wanted to tell Michael everything about Corey, especially since he'd seen him come in twice, but I feared I'd wound his ego, so I didn't.

I shook my head. "Nope."

He winked at me. "It's okay, you can tell me."

"There's nothing to tell." Though, my smile revealed otherwise. I could sense he knew I was lying.

"That's fine," Michael said. "And I won't tell you that you just got these flowers from your secret admirer." He pointed to a table in the corner on which a big bursting beautiful bouquet was awaiting.

I gasped. "Oh my God."

There was a note peeking from the bouquet. I opened it up and read the note to myself:

Lovely spending an evening with you. I hope to see you again soon. Corey

The joy I felt reading this note was overwhelming, and I swallowed the lump that was forming in my throat. Brian's voice behind me cut it short. He sounded angry. "Sam, can you come to my office?"

I turned around and walked in his direction. Michael, who stood next to the counter with puppy eyes, raised his hand as if to high-five me. As I walked by, I raised my hand and placed it in his. He gave me a gentle squeeze and a look of hope.

My heart raced. What did Brian have in store for me?

CHAPTER NINETEEN

I entered Brian's office for the very first time. The space looked like a creepy dungeon. The walls were made of brown wood panels and they diminished any daylight coming in through the single window. His desk, made of heavy steel, was a complete disaster, with papers all over it, and a desktop computer stood in a corner. The chair he was sitting on was wobbly, I could tell, as he was rocking back and forth. The heavy metal cabinets were pressed against the wall; they looked like they had been sitting there for a while. They looked heavy, as if only a crane could lift them. I wondered how Brian was spending his time here.

I couldn't imagine being in this room for ten minutes, never mind working all day in it. This room reflected Brian's personality: dark, moody, and lifeless.

Brian crossed his arms in dismissal when our eyes met. He furrowed his brows, and he made funny faces as if I disgusted him.

I planted myself on the other side of his desk and

waited for him to say something. We looked at each other in silence. Brian narrowed his eyes as if he was thinking of things to say, and nodded while pursing out his lips. I couldn't stand looking at him for one more second, so I asked, "Is there a reason you called me to your office?"

"Sam. Do you remember what I told you the day you got this job?" He sounded annoyed.

"Yes. I think I remember most of it."

"What did I tell you?" He tilted his head and squinted his eyes.

"Hm. Well, you told me I could get a discount," I quipped.

"A discount? Is that the only thing that resonated with you?"

"No, of course not." I said. "You said I should always be on time, or early, if possible."

He put a coy smile on his toothless face and said, "Now we're talking." He uncrossed his arms and put them up in the air. "So, what happened, Sam? Why are you late today?"

"It wasn't my fault. I was stuck in traffic and I had no control over it."

"Oh, really?" His voice sounded provocative.

"Really. I don't need to tell you about traffic in L.A. You know it better than me, I bet." I smiled to ease the tension.

"Let me get straight to it." He kept his gaze on me. "You're fired, Sam. You can get your stuff now and leave the premises."

"What?" The words rushed out of my mouth. "You can't fire me like this."

"I can and I am. Please leave. You are no longer an

employee of Spy Café." The way he looked at me with such hostility told me I had lost my case. To argue with Brian proved pointless. "I'll mail your last check. Or you can pick it up." He paused. "Actually, no. You should come pick it up. It will be ready for you in two days. Goodbye, Sam."

He swirled his chair around and looked through the window behind him.

I felt like someone punched me in the gut. I thought he'd complain I was late for work, but I never expected him to dismiss me like this. Both Michael and Vanessa showed up late all the time, and I mean, all the time, and he never even flinched. He must have had something personal against me, but I couldn't comprehend what. I came to work and did my job, but other than that, I'd stay out of his hair and keep my head down.

I turned around and walked away from his office. Michael saw me looking distressed and asked, "Hey, what happened?"

"I'm fired," I said with a crackly voice.

"What? Fired?" Michael's eyes were wide, his mouth agape. "But why?"

I shrugged. "No idea. For being late, I guess."

"Oh, I'm so sorry, Sam." He came in and hugged me. His hug was warm and genuine. He smelled of musky cologne mixed with sweat. I moved away from his hug and looked him in the eyes.

"Listen, I have your email and phone number. We'll stay in touch, okay?" I said.

He brightened and said, "Oh, I'd love that. I'm here if you need anything."

I tilted my head with sympathy, as I'd already decided Michael would never hear from me again. I grabbed the flowers in the corner, sniffed them once, and walked out of Spy Café without looking back.

CHAPTER TWENTY

I paced back and forth in my apartment on the day I lost my first job in L.A. My mind raced along at a thousand miles per minute. I couldn't understand what had motivated Brian to fire me like that, but my agony over it eventually turned into rage. A loud and long scream came out of me as I stood next to the window. It was echoing along the neighborhood, reaching far. Someone below yelled out, "Shut the fuck up!" I resorted back, but I had to admit screaming made me feel a lot better.

Curiosity took over. I sat down on the futon and opened up a browser on my phone. My fingers typed the search words: Brian Spy Café. I wanted to take a puzzle out of this man. Since day one, he'd acted weird. He'd looked at me and Michael strangely all the time and ordered us around even more than any other boss would. He'd stay in his office most of the time and he'd peek his head out to check what we were doing. It always irked me he'd do that. His eyes would narrow as if he was studying us and his gaze always made me uncomfortable.

The search didn't turn up much. On the first page, I found a few photos of Spy Café. The photos must have been old, because the café looked freshly painted. There were some Rio plants out front—white and red—that brightened the look of the establishment. Brian didn't care to upkeep the looks. Those photos must have been from the time someone else owned the place.

Upon scrolling down, my search revealed little about Brian. He would remain a mystery.

While typing something else, a message from Corey popped up on my phone:

Hey Sam, how's your day going?

I wasn't in a mood to talk to him, so I brushed him off by responding: Could be better.

Less than a minute passed, and his next text came through:

Uh-oh. Is there anything I can do to make it better?

I smiled. Corey knew how to make me feel better. Just as I was about to respond with another message, my phone rang. It was Corey.

"Hey, Sam. Everything okay?"

"Yeah, I'm fine. It's just that I got fired today."

"What? Fired? Are you serious?" Corey sounded concerned.

"Yep. Fired."

"But why?"

"I was late for work this morning, because I slept in at your house." I let out a laugh.

"Oh, yes. So, I guess it's all my fault." He paused. "I'm so sorry, Sam."

"It's not your fault. You had nothing to do with me falling asleep like that. Don't blame yourself."

"Phew," he said. "I'm glad to hear that. But, you know, I still feel bad about you losing your job. I'm a little responsible. No?"

"It's okay, really."

"Sam? How about I pick you up tonight and we go for a walk near my house? There's a pleasant path that leads to the woods. We don't need to go far."

I reached for the seam of my dress and swirled it around with my index finger. Whenever I had to think hard, I'd always occupy my hands with a mindless task. I closed my eyes and shook my head to get rid of the internal conflict raging inside me. Corey was wonderful, a dream even, but I didn't know him very well. I didn't want Corey to think I was taking advantage.

"Sam?" Corey said.

"Yes. Okay. Sure. Come pick me up."

I could hear his smile. "Wonderful. I'll see you around six."

At six, I was standing at the curb, waiting for the BMW to show up. When Corey failed to show up ten minutes later, I paced up and down. Perhaps he changed his mind, and no longer wanted to see me tonight? Perhaps the traffic was heavy even though it was past rush hour time. You never knew in L.A. When twenty minutes passed, betting on the fact he was still alive and safe, my concern turned into annoyance. He could have at least called me to give me a heads up.

At last, the BMW stopped in front of me. Corey looked concerned, but when our eyes locked, he smiled.

"Sorry for running late. I had to do a quick errand, and I lost track of time." He waved his hand. "Come on in."

"No worries." I smiled. "It's good to see you."

I hid my annoyance. Acting was my passion, and I used it with every opportunity.

Corey took me out to a restaurant as opposed to a walk. He said he hadn't eaten all day and was starving. We sat at the restaurant table and the waiter came and took our order, and Corey couldn't seem to take his eyes off me.

"Thanks for the flowers." I interrupted his gaze.

He lowered his head. "You're most welcome. I enjoyed our evening last night and thought I'd let you know by sending you the flowers."

"How thoughtful." I smiled. "I enjoyed our evening as well."

He then inquired about my job loss. I told him about Brian and how confusing the whole thing was. He looked at me and said, "I know you can do better than that place. I have faith something better would show up soon."

"You do?"

"Yes. Until your acting career takes off."

"About that..." I didn't want to press the issue, but I needed to know if he made any progress in reaching his friend Chris. "Have you spoken with your friend yet?"

"Who? Chris?" Corey said.

No. Donald Duck. "Yes. Chris." I smiled to conceal my anger.

"I texted him this morning, and I'm still waiting to hear back. That's Chris, you know. I sometimes wait months for him to get back, but he does eventually." He must have sensed my anxiety. "Why? Are you worried about this?"

I shook my head and looked down. "I hope to talk to someone—anyone—who can help me get my feet wet with acting." I looked up at Corey. "I… I don't know. My rent is high, and I don't know how much longer I can stay in my apartment. I need to find something pronto, and I prefer acting over any other job."

"Of course." He slumped in his chair.

Corey looked at me with all seriousness and proposed the question I didn't see coming. "Sam." He fidgeted in his seat, then froze in place. "I told you I traveled a lot for work. I'd say I spend eighty percent of my time outside my home. My job is quite demanding… and so, I'm wondering if you'd be willing to be my roommate?"

"Your roommate?" I repeated. My chest filled with warmth and a million butterflies vied for attention in my stomach. This had to be a dream. Right?

Corey nodded and smiled. "My house would feel live-lier and different if you lived there. You'd have it all to yourself and you can stay there until you find a job that you love. The entire left wing can be all yours."

It's as if someone just slapped me, but in a good way. I'd move out of that small apartment and never listen to gunshots or my upstairs neighbor again.

I didn't want to sound eager. "Let me think about it. I appreciate your generous offer."

Corey changed his face expression, as if feeling embar-rassed about what he had just proposed. He quickly changed the topic, and I felt bad about reducing him to shame.

I looked around, as if seeking an exit, and announced I had to run to the bathroom. When I arrived, I plunged myself above the sink and stared at myself in the mirror. Fear crossed my face as thoughts ran through my mind. I didn't understand what prompted Corey to extend such a generous offer. We had known each other for a few days, and it seemed too good to be true. I never trusted people who gave so easily. Were they in a state of despair my presence would help fix?

I was pondering too much.

My eyes returned to a normal state. This couldn't be so bad, I thought. There was nothing wrong with extending generosity; it could be easier to do so for people with means than those without. Corey had a big house he barely spent time in. I had to trust my gut and go with it. My lips cracked into a smile. I turned around and exited through the door.

When I sat back down at the table, I smiled at Corey and announced, "I've already decided. When can I move in?"

CHAPTER TWENTY-ONE

Corey was nothing like my father. Corey's smile was a stark difference from my father's furrowed brows. He seemed to care about people, unlike my father, who'd lost interest in his daughter at her early age. I'd yearned for his love.

I'd longed for the sort of father he'd been when my grandparents were still around. It was as if he wanted to prove to them he could be a good parent. He'd often take me out for walks or to a pizza joint down the street. In the summer, a Ferris wheel would come to Gallup and he'd take me there on the opening day. I was his little princess, as he sometimes called me back then before everything went so very wrong.

When my father distanced himself from us, I watched him transform into a physically repulsive being. He no longer smiled, and no longer had anything positive to say. He'd still arrive home from work at a decent time, but all he did was complain for the rest of the evening until I was ushered off to bed. One evening, just as I fell asleep, the sound of the Moonlight Sonata woke me up. The music was blasting through the house, but my mother's screams and cries rose above it. An occasional scream from my father vibrated in my ears, but nothing struck me as awful as my mother's cries.

My mother was weak and vulnerable, never having the guts to leave my father or, at the least, confront him. Her sanctuary was the Church where my father's sins became hers at the confession stand. She took father's behaviors too personally and blamed herself for it. I despised my mother's weakness. I knew I was losing both of them at a rapid speed.

Shame and guilt became a collective order in our household. Everyone in Gallup knew that my parents' marriage spiraled down to a deep abyss. The Church ladies my mother once became close to now stayed away from her in the fear my mother's ill fate would rub off on them. Isolated, my mother kept defending Father and saying he was a good man. She was hoping for him to turn around, which to me would be nothing short of a miracle.

One night, Father came home, kicking his boots in the living room and putting his feet on the coffee table. He didn't bother to say hello or inquire about our day. He turned the TV on and put the volume at a maximum. My mother stormed out of the room and went to the kitchen; I could sense she was hiding there with tears in her eyes. I sat down across from my father in a recliner chair—the one my grandfather used to rock on all the time—and waited for an opportune moment to remind my father my sixth birthday was coming up. Just as I was about to say something, I noticed he had a bottle of beer in his hand. His eyes looked heavy, as if he was about to fall asleep.

When he'd taken a sip of his beer, I jumped up from the recliner and approached my father. The closer I got, the more pungent the alcohol coming out of his body was. I came up to him, expecting a hug, a caress. Instead, my father raised his hand and smacked me on my left cheek. I clearly remembered it was a left cheek, because I no longer felt that side of my body. The pain throbbed. I watched Father turn his attention to the TV while I stood there, motionless. I had hoped my father made a mistake and didn't mean to hit me, but his voice exacerbated my shock.

"What do you want?" he mumbled in his heavy, raspy voice.

I wanted to cry, but tears didn't want to come out. It was at that moment that Father chipped away my innocence. I looked at him through narrowed eyes and whispered, "I want you to die."

CHAPTER TWENTY-TWO

Corey insisted I move to his house the following day, even though I could wait for my month-to-month lease to expire. It sounded better to move to Corey's place and get away from the sketchy neighborhood for good.

The timing of my move was perfect, because the day it happened, my upstairs neighbor rehearsed with his drummer. Madness and anger oozed from the sound of the heavy metal music. It surprised me that the building management would allow these rehearsals, but I no longer had a dog in this fight. Now they could do whatever they wanted.

I had nothing but my luggage to move, which consisted mostly of clothes. Before I moved to L.A., my mother took me to a strip mall and had me pick out a few dresses for the trip—her treat. They were for good luck; she said. I was yet to see it. But maybe luck had finally knocked on my door, as I imagined living in the enormity of Corey's home.

When Corey drove me to my new home, silence fell

between us. What was going on in Corey's mind? Had he realized that my moving into his house was too soon? Did he regret his decision? When we stopped at a light, he looked at me and smiled without saying a word.

His residence was remote from the city, even more so than I'd realized. As we drove further, the landscape changed like a cascade on a painting. We were now surrounded by hills and trees, and there were only a few cars or people around. The closest strip mall, I surmised, was several miles away. Without a car, it would be a long walk.

As Corey drove onto the private passage leading to his house, the gravel underneath the tires crunched beneath, killing our silence.

The gate opened up, and the car advanced to the front of the house where Corey parked on the cul-de-sac. We rushed out of the car.

Corey opened the front door and ushered me inside. "Welcome home."

I dragged the luggage behind me and felt just as in awe of the house as I had been last time. This time I was viewing it as a home, and it was almost as if I was seeing it once again for the first time. Every corner, every detail wowed me, and my excitement at knowing that this was my new habitat was palpable.

Corey lifted his index finger and wagged it like a little tail, signaling me to follow him. As we walked, I thought all of this must have been a dream; a dream I'd wake up from before finding myself on an old futon in the loud studio apartment.

We walked up the stairs to the second floor. We passed two doors on the right and two on the left until he opened

the door in the far-right corner. "Here it is. Your room."
He extended his arm and gestured it like he was
announcing a stage performer.

I'd slept in the same room the night before. It occurred
to me that the bedroom hadn't been used much. Despite
its underuse, it was neat and dust-free. My former studio
apartment was the same size. Satin sheets covered the bed;
the elegant drapes enveloped the windows; the carpet and
the walls were of the matching colors. A giant bathroom
with marble floors was next to the bedroom. I was
breathless.

"Oh my God, Corey. This is so beautiful." I walked up
to him and gave him a hug. "How could I ever thank
you?"

He squeezed me around my waist and buried his nose
in my hair. "You're welcome, sweetheart. Hope you feel at
home." He weaseled himself out of my hug and turned
around. "Why don't you make yourself comfortable before
we have dinner tonight?"

"Okay." I felt warmth and joy inside. I hadn't felt like
this since my grandparents were alive. They made our
house inviting and homely, always smelling of cooked food
prepared by Grandmother.

As Corey left my room, he slammed the door. I jumped
and cringed at the sound. He probably didn't mean to, but
he didn't come back to apologize.

My room looked as if it came from an interior design
magazine, but something was off. When I realized the
room smelled of old vomit beyond the lavender that was
trying to mask it, I crinkled my nose. The room hadn't
been occupied in so long that it hadn't been aired out
recently. That must be it. I cracked one window open and

the heat splashed me. It wasn't even summer yet, and the days had already become super hot.

I sat on the bed to compose my thoughts. I felt overwhelmed and out of place, as if someone else was having these experiences. As I stared at the window, a little tiny object sitting on the windowsill drew my attention. I walked up to the window and saw a white baby monitor. It was not plugged in or didn't seem to work. I wondered what the baby monitor was doing in one of Corey's bedroom. I could only solve the mystery with a simple, casual question to Corey. But Mother would have something to say about that.

When Michelle and I were little, she gave me a friendship bracelet for my sixth birthday. She had not mastered the craft, so the bracelet had turned out quite unattractive. I didn't want to hurt her feelings, but I'd complained. "Mom, I don't want to wear this. It's too ugly."

My church-going mother said, "Sam, don't look a gift horse in the mouth."

"What horse?" I looked around, searching for one.

Mother laughed. "It's a saying."

"What does it mean?" I asked.

"It means you should be grateful for someone's generosity." Silence ensued.

"Even when I don't deserve it?"

Mom said with confidence: "Especially when you don't deserve it."

CHAPTER TWENTY-THREE

Corey's generosity entered my life while it was upside down. I had no prospects, no job, and no safe apartment. It was easy for me to enter his life—it gave me hope mine would turn for the better. He'd be physically absent a lot, but being alone in a suitable home would give me the opportunity to reassess my options.

Corey said his busiest flying months were in the summer when air traffic thickened with enthused passengers to reach a paradise destination or reunite with their loved ones. There was something about summer that made people want to move about more than usual. He meant I'd spend most of the summer in the house alone.

Dinner was waiting on the dining room table when I arrived downstairs. Corey was preparing something in the kitchen and the smell of the food made me realize I was hungry. I entered the kitchen and when Corey saw me, he exclaimed, "Hey, perfect timing. The dinner is ready."

He stood in the middle of the kitchen, looking at me and taking off his apron. His biceps under his t-shirt looked about to burst. He smiled at me and pointed at the dining table that was over ten feet long. I sat down while Corey brought the food to the table, looking focused. He shut everything in the kitchen and came to sit at the table next to me.

The meal he prepared looked delicious: mashed potatoes, a salad, steak, and some sort of gravy on the side. I couldn't help but question if there was anything wrong with this man. He seemed perfect, and he made me feel safe.

We ate in silence. Corey cut his steak with a knife and place a piece in his mouth delicately. I tried to catch his gaze, but he was too focused on his food.

"Where did you learn how to cook so well?" I said.

He smiled. Before he spoke, he grabbed the napkin from his lap and tapped his mouth a few times to wipe it. "When my mom was still alive, she taught me how to cook. She cooked every day and was quite good at it."

"Oh, I'm sorry. I didn't know your mom was no longer with us."

"Don't worry. I don't talk about my parents often." He gazed down and kept his gaze for a long while. "Anyway, they're both gone."

"I'm glad she left a legacy behind. You are a superb cook." I said and dove into my steak.

A sense of guilt washed over me when I realized I'd never cook for Corey. That was one skill I'd never developed. I could make myself a sandwich, boil eggs, make coffee, but beyond that, the kitchen wasn't my friend. My mother, being so busy with her drugs, never showed me how meals were prepared. She wasn't much of a cook herself, though. She knew how to make eggs the best—low and slow—a great recipe her friend Freida once gave her, and she made them often enough that they would become our regular diet. So, when someone cooked for me beyond just scrambled eggs, I'd see it as a noble gesture. Like I owed that person something in return.

I took Corey's hand and squeezed it. To my surprise, he yanked it out of my hand and returned to eating his steak. Perhaps it was a delicate topic he didn't want me to talk about, and I decided I'd never mention his parents again.

As time went on, only the sound of the cutlery filled the void between us. A thousand thoughts and questions filled my mind, but I had no strength to raise them. Corey seemed like a bit of a puzzle that I couldn't place in my mind.

When we finished eating, Corey grabbed the napkin and put it on the table. He placed his elbows on the table-top, crossed his hands and rested his chin on his hands. His eyes gazed at me and his lips formed a smile.

"Sam, remember this is your home now, until you find something more suitable. You can stay as long as you want." He turned around and extended his arm toward the kitchen. "That pantry over there is packed with food. You won't need to go grocery shopping for the next six months. Unless you want something in particular. But I doubt you won't find it here."

"Seriously? No grocery shopping for the whole six months?" My eyes widened. "Why do you buy so much food when you barely live here?"

He paused and grabbed the napkin. I noticed he squeezed it hard, as if he was about to strangle it.

"I like my house to be stock-piled. It's a good feeling

when you return home from travels and everything is here." He rose from the chair and continued, "Anyway, I should go to bed now. I have to get up early and fly to Argentina."

Why Argentina? I wouldn't dare ask.

"I'll be in touch as often as I can." He stood in the kitchen, stiff like a soldier in a line of duty. "I will see you in a week if nothing gets complicated."

I followed him with my eyes as he was walking toward his bedroom.

"Hey, Corey." I said.

He turned around on his heels and looked at me with wide eyes. "What?"

"Before you leave, do you mind giving me the Wi-Fi password for the house?"

"Sorry, there's no Wi-Fi here."

"No Wi-Fi? But the phone connection in the house is terrible. I've got, like, one bar. How am I going to keep in touch with everyone?"

He shrugged. "No idea."

With that, Corey turned around and walked away into the dark hallway.

CHAPTER TWENTY-FOUR

I tossed and turned in my bed all night. Sleep didn't come, as too many thoughts occupied my mind. It must have been four in the morning when my eyes felt heavy and tired enough to give up and take me to dreamland.

By the time I woke up, Corey had already left. I peeked through the window and noticed his BMW was no longer parked there. On my right side sat a closet, which made me happy. Back home in Gallup, my room in the apartment my mother rented was small, and so was the closet.

I opened up the closet in my new room and marveled at it. On the right side were shelves, spaced out evenly between each other. On the left side was a rod to hang things. I moved my luggage closer to the closet. One by one, I took the clothing items out of my luggage and placed them on the shelf as if made of glass. It felt good to be settling in one place where space was plenty.

I left my room and found myself in the kitchen. The fancy coffee maker drew my immediate attention, and I brewed myself a strong cup of coffee. Nothing like caffeine to perk me up.

The French door leading to the backyard was wide open, letting warmth and sunshine in. With a cup of coffee in my hand, I walked outside and took a seat on a giant outdoor couch overlooking the nearby pool. It was so peaceful, I could hear my breathing. But there was something about hearing my breathing—it was drawing out fear of being alone; fear of having too much time on my hands to think; fear of not having a clear future ahead.

I had to keep myself busy.

I entered the house and looked to my right and then to my left. The right wing and the left wing. Like a detective, I walked in slow motion, as if expecting someone to come out and attack me. The house was quiet except for the refrigerator gently buzzing. On the first floor were the guest room, kitchen and the dining room, all in one open space. As I exited the guest room, I found myself in the narrow hallway in the right wing, with a bathroom on one side and a primary bedroom on the other side. That was where Corey slept. I wanted to enter his room and snoop around, but I feared a house like this one would have hidden cameras all over.

I swallowed my temptation and turned around to see what was on the other side of the kitchen. Leading down another narrow hallway, I found myself in front of a door that I thought I heard strange sounds coming from— something like howling. I placed my ear close to the door and focused on it, but the howling was gone.

My hand grabbed for the doorknob and gently twisted it to the right. The door opened and only darkness dominated the space. I put my hand on the wall to find the light switch and, when I did and the lights came on, I stood there, stunned.

"Wow." I'd seen nothing like this before. A TV screen the size of a wall was at the end of the room. Several comfortable recliner chairs were spaced perfectly like this was a class A theater. I could spend most of my time here and watch movies and study my favorite actors.

After I wowed the room, I went upstairs to continue exploring my new home. My bedroom was in the far right corner upstairs, but what was in the other three rooms? I opened up the door for the first room and, with renewed anticipation, I expected to see something unusual. But when I opened the door, I saw a bed and a dresser, much resembling my room. How many times had it been used? How many guests had Corey had? Did he have other random people, like me, live in his house on a whim?

I closed the door and checked out the room across the way. Same thing. Just another unused bedroom. They all looked beautifully decorated.

Finding out what was in the last room across from mine would be the last task for the day. I came up to the door and casually twisted the doorknob, only to discover the door was locked. It was rather strange that, of all the rooms, this bedroom was inaccessible. What was inside? Was Corey hiding something? I grabbed the doorknob a little tighter and twisted it on both sides, but the door wouldn't budge. As I was about to quit, I looked down and something drew my attention. It looked like someone had tried to break into this bedroom before. The door was destroyed a few inches near the doorknob, as if someone chipped it with a knife. I put my hand on the chipped hole as if to examine its age, but it was difficult to tell when the offender might have tried to break in.

I kneeled down and placed my head on the floor, looking at the crevice between the ground and the door. The room was pitch black and no sign of life was coming from the space. What was Corey hiding in this room? And if there was something significant, who wanted it? And why?

Unease rose inside me, and I shook my head to dislodge the sudden sense of foreboding.

CHAPTER TWENTY-FIVE

Despite the mystery surrounding the locked room, the house grew on me and made me feel comfortable. But the dead silence irked me. When my mother spent countless times in a rehab, I spent most of my time alone, but I never felt lonely. Surrounded by my neighbors in the two-story apartment building, they often knocked on my door to check up on me. Ms. Harris down the hall shared the food with me every day. I'd greet her at the door, take the food, and walk to the kitchen to toss it in the trash. Her casserole looked disgusting, and her pies mushed. Michelle often came to visit, and she and I would order a pizza with the money her parents gave her as a weekly allowance. That was the only time I was jealous of her—her parents spent money on her, my mother spent her money on drugs.

There was something inhumane about being alone in large spaces. I felt like I was the only person left on the planet. Exploring the house was exciting initially, but as it wore off, my boredom became prominent. I swam in the pool, but even then, the heat became unbearable, and I'd hide in the house.

My phone was the only connection with the rest of the world. The TV seemed to have a couple of local channels featuring news all the time. That world didn't interest me, so I kept the TV off.

I found a selfie of me in a bikini I'd taken earlier on my phone and sent it to Corey with a simple X next to it. A hug. That was good. Unassuming and unpretentious. My phone had only one bar, so I stared down at the screen until the selfie finally reached Corey. When the message appeared delivered, I continued to stare, thinking Corey would respond immediately as he always did, but nothing was coming through.

I reckoned Corey was busy. His lack of immediate response shouldn't concern me. Besides, we were only roommates, and he owed me nothing. I owed him everything. But, being alone, when nobody was there to validate or reason my thoughts and feelings, only dark thoughts come to mind. They distracted and scared me. Many what-ifs crossed my mind. What if something happened to Corey? What if nothing happened to him, but he regretted his decision to have me move into his house? What if my selfie was too provocative, and he didn't want to respond to lead me on?

I dialed Michelle to find out what she was up to. After a second ring, she answered the phone. She sounded upset as soon as she spoke.

"Dude, where have you been?" She always called me dude when she was angry with me. "I've tried to call you so many times the past couple of days, but your phone kept going to voicemail. What is happening, Sam?"

"Everything's okay." I added a smile she could sense to calm her down. "I don't have the best reception where I am right now."

"Where are you?"

"I moved yesterday. I no longer live in the studio apartment."

"You did? Where do you live now?"

"Michelle, you'd never believe the house I live in. It is giant, with a swimming pool and a tennis court." These words caused an unsettling feeling and cut through my stomach. I wondered if I'd made a mistake in taking up Corey on his generous offer. Something felt off, but I couldn't put my finger on it.

"Oh," was all Michelle could muster.

"Don't worry. It's just temporary until I get a permanent acting gig. There's nothing to worry about. You should come visit me soon."

Beep beep beep.

We lost the connection. The one bar on my phone turned into none. I dialed Michelle several times, but I couldn't connect. I wanted to give her my new address, but then I realized I didn't know what it was.

I started moving around the house to find any mail Corey might have received in the past several weeks, but I saw nothing on the tops of any desks or tables. Eventually, I found a small pile of mail when I opened the drawers in the hallway. I picked it up and saw a piece of junk mail—a moving company—addressed to someone named Michael Corrigan.

Michael Corrigan? The name sounded familiar until the image of Michael from Spy Café came to mind. Wasn't his name Michael Corrigan?

All this could be just a coincidence. There had to be hundreds of Michael Corrigans out there. It was perhaps Corey's brother or a cousin who might have lived here temporarily at some point. Hence the mail tucked in the drawer.

I wanted to believe this was true until it hit me: I didn't even know Corey's last name. The unsettling feeling grew more. I had so many questions for Corey once I saw him again.

CHAPTER TWENTY-SIX

My days had no feel to them. Usually, Sundays bred nostalgia or Mondays were mundane. Every day resembled the previous one. Corey never responded to my text, and if he did, it didn't reach me. I had tried dialing Michelle several times already, but I kept getting her voicemail. My phone proved to be useless. Silence was killing me. Every time I turned the TV on, a news anchor talked about a war.

Today, the Russian air missiles struck civilian targets in the eastern part of Ukraine. More than a dozen people, including children, have been killed...

I turned off the TV. Savages. Wars didn't interest me; it was enough I was fighting my battles inside.

Boredom crept in. Having a large house with all the fancy amenities meant nothing when you could share it with nobody. The house turned into a sad display of luxury and grandeur. Corey had no books in the house.

I went to my room and lied down on the bed, staring at the ceiling. My mind raced as I contemplated my next steps. I had to get out of the house and venture out to the town to look for a job. Any job would do it. I didn't want Corey to think I depended on him. A big part of me wanted to prove that I could take care of myself. Now that I was almost twenty, adulthood had to make me self-reliant and responsible.

I twitched. A loud thump echoed along the hallway, but I couldn't tell if the source came from inside or outside the house. I grabbed the covers and pulled them to my chin. What was that? My eyes widened out of fear that someone could have broken in. Maybe Corey came back from his trip early. Silence returned after I held my breath and listened to other sounds. I let time go by until I mustered the courage to get up and leave my room.

I walked down the hall and peeked over the railing to see any evidence of the break-in, but everything seemed intact. The house looked normal and untouched. I walked down the stairs and, at the bottom of the stairway, I looked to my left and right, only to see the long hallway. No other lifeform presented itself.

The weather outside seeped brightness and peace. The green lawn was cut, and the hedges along the fence were trimmed to perfection. I wondered how often Corey would have his lawn tended to since it was pointless when he wasn't here long enough to enjoy it. I took a few steps along the house and noticed something lying in the grass. Something gray. I couldn't quite discern what it was. When I approached it, I realized it was a dead bird. It wasn't a sparrow; it was too large. I looked up at the house and noticed a smudge on one window. The bird must have hit the window and fallen into its immediate death in the grass.

I picked it up at the edge of its one wing and moved it to the fence near the entrance gate. I kneeled down and dug up a hole, making a makeshift grave for the bird. The hole was deep enough to become the bird's permanent home. I placed it in the hole and covered it up with the dirt. My hands automatically moved to my face, and I placed my palms together. While my eyes were closed, I whispered a prayer my grandmother taught me when I was a young child.

As my eyes remained closed, I whispered another prayer. I prayed that my life would turn around soon. That my acting career would take off. That I would find a permanent home soon.

When I opened my eyes, I cringed at the brightness. I looked up at the entrance gate and I stood up, quickening my steps toward it. A small box was next to it, and I opened it to discover the dial box. I searched for my memory until Corey's note appeared in front of my eyes: "the code for the gate is 1115."

I pushed those four digits, but with the speed, I missed one and a little lamp flashed red. The code was wrong. I dialed again 1-1-1-5 and, like the heavens opening up, the gate's doors inched until they were wide open. Paralyzed, I stood in front of it. Now was my chance to run away and never return to this place. I could find help from the outside. But who was I kidding? The world wasn't as kind as I imagined it to be. Instead, a walk to clear my head would diminish this feeling of anguish. I turned around and walked into the house to get myself ready for a long walk.

CHAPTER TWENTY-SEVEN

Corey didn't exaggerate about the amount of food in the house. I didn't need to see a grocery store for a whole six months. Or longer. The food was plenty. It felt like a nuclear missile was about to strike, and all the preparation for it took in the form of collecting food. The pantry that Corey pointed out before he left was a size of a small room. On one side of the wall was a long fridge and a freezer with the food labeled across the shelves—POUL-TRY, BEEF, FISH, PREMADE MEALS—and on the other side of the wall were cans upon cans and jars upon jars of vegetables, fruits, beans, pickles, jams of different flavors. My eyes glazed over it. I'd been overwhelmed at the sight the first time I'd gone in there, but I was getting used to the sense of abundance by now. All I wanted was a bottle of still water.

I looked down and saw dozens of bottled waters and soft drinks. I took one and put it in my purse. The day wasn't as hot as previous ones, but water down the road would be more than welcome. On my way out, I grabbed a granola bar to keep my strength up on my walk.

I headed out and felt liberated to walk through the gates, which were still wide open. The house was so off grid I didn't think that any stranger or passers-by would venture this way and try to break in. Only people who knew the house existed would succumb to that temptation.

The road leading from the house was quiet. When I came to the end of the private path, I stood for a few seconds, deciding whether to take a left or a right. What awaited miles away could only be a guess, but I'd follow my instinct and take a right. I walked through a residential area with houses as big as Corey's. It was the part of L.A. reserved for the upper class. The hedges along the fences were carefully tended. The palm trees extended high and gave a decorative sense to the neighbors' yards.

Walking along such a quiet street had lulled me into a false sense of security, and I was startled when I heard the long honk of a horn and the screeching of brakes. I whipped around and froze in place for a moment as a red car came hurtling towards me, stopping just inches away from my quivering body.

"Either stop walking in the middle of the road or watch where you're going," the driver yelled through his window as he rushed past. He offered no apology for his ridiculously high speed in a residential area. I should have taken his license plate, but everything happened so fast.

My legs wobbled beneath me, and I slumped down on the side of the road. Seeing that car careening towards me so seemingly out of control reminded me of another day. Another Car. My father's lifeless body.

I was six-years old. My mother prepared lunch for me and helped me put my school clothes on. She walked me to the car and gave me a kiss on the forehead. My father sat at the wheel in front of me; he'd woken up rather grumpy that morning. But it did not differ from any other day. He and my mother fought the night before; I heard them through my bedroom wall. I never knew what the source of the contention was, but the sound traveling to my ears echoed for a long time. If I were to choose my parents' relationship, they would have filled it with love and harmony. It was far from that.

I was sitting behind my father while I stared at his balding spot in the back. The fights with my mother took a toll on him and he was aging faster than he should have. Over time, he'd become distant and disinterested in spending time with me. I wanted to be Dad's little princess he'd most lovingly adore again, but the look on his face every time I asked him to read me a book repelled me and drew me closer into my shell. My father was now just a wax figure who had no interest in making my mom or me happy.

I resented him for that. His balding spot looked deformed and ugly. I still couldn't explain what came over me, what forced me to pick up the metal object sitting next to me, but I grabbed it and with all my might struck my father in the bald spot.

"God damn it!" My father screamed, and his voice seemed louder in the confined space of the car. He temporarily lost control of the wheel from the shock of the strike and began weaving on the road. What happened next escaped my memory, because it all happened so fast. I recalled the car heading for a corner building and jamming into the bricks. My father's head was now further away, resting on the wheel, blood oozing from it. I wasn't sure if the next sound was the car alarm or my ears buzzing, but it was loud and made my head hurt. A police car showed up shortly after, and one cop opened the back passenger door to rescue me. She had a concerned look on her face and asked me if I was okay. The buzzing noise in my ears muffled her voice.

An ambulance car showed a few minutes later. Two technicians wheeled a stretcher out and to my father's side of the car. A female cop opened up my door and took me in her arms. She put me down on the ground, unconcerned I was watching my father unconscious and bloody. I stared up at the gray sky. One of the EMT people shouted, giving the instructions to the other. His voice sounded alarmed and panicky. Was Father not going to make it? They put him down on the stretcher and rushed him into the ambulance car.

I didn't mean for any of this to happen. I didn't realize hitting my father with an object would cause him to run into a building. The ambulance drove him fast to the hospital; the alarm whirring through the town. My mother appeared out of nowhere and gave me a hug. Her eyes filled with tears. I expected her to thank me for teaching Father a lesson. But none of that happened. She cried all day and night, and she prayed for him. The following day, my mother came up to me, sobbing.

"Your father died," she said. All day long, she didn't stop sobbing.

He died in the hospital the following day.

Had I known my mother would grieve so much with Father gone, I would have reconsidered my action. An indescribable amount of guilt filled me. Not only because I was now a child capable of murder but also because I'd made my Mother suffer even more.

Everything changed. I was no longer an innocent six-year-old.

Ever since my father died in the car crash, I hadn't wanted to be myself. I didn't want to live in my body and flesh. Guilt attached to me like a malevolent bracelet charm. From then on, I vowed to spend my life pretending to be someone else. Anyone else. The stage or the studio would be the answer. Somewhere I could hide the real me. Father's voice reverberated in my head, leading me to an internal void that seemed to last forever.

CHAPTER TWENTY-EIGHT

When I got to the strip mall, I snapped out of my thoughts. I might have walked a couple of miles straight. I didn't feel any soreness in my feet, considering I had moved little in the recent days. Beyond the first few blocks, I paid little attention to my surroundings. I loved seeing people around. They seemed unfazed and minding their own business. At the mall, most stores were mom-and-pop shops. They looked deserted from the outside as no one walked through the doors. One store held a sign: HIRING IMMEDIATELY. APPLY WITHIN.

I walked through the door and found myself inside an unusual store that was selling trinkets, toys, magazines, books, T-shirts—an assortment of items. The store had no customers, and it smelled of old carpet.

A woman behind the counter, sitting in a low chair, looked up from her book and greeted me. "Can I help you?" She sounded annoyed.

"Hi. Your store is adorable." I said. I yearned for a

conversation. It was difficult to admit, but I missed the human connection. Being alone in the house for days built an urge to talk.

"Thanks." She put her head down and continued reading. Her red curly hair stood out like a clown's. She had no visible interest in engaging with me or showcasing any customer service skills.

I walked and made a circle around a stack of shelves in the middle of the store. Dozens of used books sat on the shelves. My mother hadn't bought me many books growing up, so I'd make frequent trips to the school library. Teachers couldn't understand my love for the written word given my mediocre grades. They couldn't understand anything about me. For them, I was an enigma.

I picked up a book from a shelf, Frankenstein by Mary Shelley, and flipped it over. The smell of old paper splashed over me as I read. The redhead beyond the counter asked me no questions. I turned in her direction to see her in the same position with the same face expression. She'd immersed herself in the book in her hands.

"What are you reading?" I said.

She looked up and grimaced.

"It's Neil Gaiman." she said and put her head down.

I approached the counter and, as my shadow covered her, she looked up at me with terrified eyes. "Can I help you with something?"

"I have a question." I used a gentle voice not to scare or annoy her further. "There's a sign on the window saying you're hiring. Is... is the position still open?"

"Yes."

"If that's the case, I'd like to apply."

She crinkled her nose and measured me up and down. "Do you have retail experience?"

"Well. Some. I just had a job in a coffee shop, if that counts."

"Had? What happened?"

"Well." My heart raced. "It didn't work out."

"You got fired, didn't you?"

"I did." I said calmly, concealing my fear.

"Yeah. I know your type." She put her head down and ignored me.

"You're saying I shouldn't bother applying?" I knew the answer, but I wanted confirmation of sorts.

She looked up, with rage in her eyes, and put her head down without saying a word.

I shook my head in dismay and turned around. I walked through the door without saying goodbye.

Disappointed by the fruitless exchange and the failed attempt at finding a job, I headed back home. When I approached the major intersection, I noticed a white BMW stopped at the light. It made me think of Corey and his white BMW that he seemed so proud of. As I stared at the car a little longer, I recognized the driver's profile sitting at the wheel. His contours were familiar until it hit me that the person behind the wheel had to be Corey. I rubbed my eyes like a character in a cartoon to see better. Corey was sitting at the wheel, talking and laughing. He had to be on the phone, hands-free, since he was in the car alone. The traffic light turned green, and the car headed in the opposite direction from Corey's house.

Standing there stunned, I yelled out, "Corey!"

But my voice couldn't reach the car. Corey was supposed to be in Argentina. Was I hallucinating? It was possible loneliness was playing with my mind. But it was also possible that my visions and voices had returned after so many years. The first time they came was when Father died.

Why had they returned?

CHAPTER TWENTY-NINE

Last time I saw visions was in the psych ward. My mother thought it was a good idea for me to be evaluated based on the first vision of Father in my room. He'd appeared out of nowhere, sat down on my bed, and chatted to me. Unlike the way I remembered him, he was laughing, and he seemed happy to see me. At the psych ward, he followed me everywhere, watching every move I made. In my room, he'd sit next to me and stare into my eyes. Sometimes, we'd have long conversations, but we'd whisper out of fear in case the chief psychologist came over and discovered Father.

Distraught by the unexpected sight of Corey, my feet couldn't carry me home fast enough, and I kept stumbling. The houses, people, trees, cars—everything became a blur. On the private path, I tripped and fell down, burning my palms and knees. The fall was hard, but I stood up, dusted myself off, and ran to the house. When I reached the house, I expected to see Corey's BMW parked in front of it. There were no traces of the car or him. The house looked as I'd left it.

I entered the house and reached for my phone. It occurred to me that Corey had never responded to my text from a few days ago. I wanted to believe he was too busy or had no opportunity to get back to me, but my reality was now distorted and skewed. If that was him in the car, then Corey had to be busy hiding something.

My phone had only one bar. But it was still possible to transmit texts, even though it took forever. I found Michael's contact and typed in a message:

Hey, Michael. Hope you're good. I need to ask a favor of you.

I had thought I would never see or contact Michael again, but beggars can't be choosers. Michael could help me find the truth. I remembered he was a freelance writer, and his research capabilities could come in handy.

The message went through. My hands shook. I stared at my phone, but my message failed to get delivered. Maybe Michael turned off his phone, and the text would be delivered when he turned it back on. Michael was always responsive. Although I didn't want to go out on dates with him, I believed in my heart that he wanted us to be friends.

I went about my business, checking my phone as often as I could muster. By the evening, my message to Michael still hadn't been delivered, so I frantically searched through my contacts until I found Vanessa's phone number. I clicked on her name and typed. It was my first message ever to her.

Hey Vanessa, it's Sam. Mind sending me Michael's contact info?

The message was transmitted slowly, but it was ultimately delivered.

Five minutes later, my phone bleeped. A message from Vanessa. She had only attached Michael's contact information from her phone and didn't say a word.

I clicked on it and compared the numbers I already had for Michael. They were identical. It was unlike Michael not to respond for hours at a time or to keep his phone off. I knew that much about Michael, because he was almost always on the phone, playing Candy Crush or reading the daily news when Spy Café was slow. I thought of the possibility that he'd blocked me, but I couldn't reason why.

I sat on the couch of the guest room and racked my brain. Nothing came to mind.

CHAPTER THIRTY

Two or three days had passed since I thought I saw Corey in town. I spent most of my time at the pool, sitting on the chair, lifeless, waiting for a sign. The sun burned my skin, but I didn't care. Nothing made sense anymore. My phone died a long ago after my charger mysteriously went missing. Even one bar never returned. Venturing out and being among people would make a difference, but I feared interactions with people.

July 15th was my birthday. I didn't know if it already came or was still coming. I only knew that it didn't feel any different from the previous years. My only memory of a joyful celebration of my life was when my grandparents were alive. I couldn't have been more than four at the time. Grandmother prepared a cake and placed it in the middle of the table after dinner. We looked at it in silence, waiting for Grandmother to cut and slice it. Having candles wasn't part of the deal. I had seen a child blowing them in commercials and I had wished I was that child. My grandmother would start singing happy birthday, and everyone but Father joined in. He looked at me in silence, smiling, although I could sense he wasn't there a hundred percent. Later, I wondered if that was when the troubles with my parents began.

After that year, my birthdays didn't get any special notice. My father, two years in a row until his death, would forget it, while my mother would recall it a few days later. She'd buy me a crazy number of presents, feeling guilty. After Father died, my mother stopped remembering my birthday altogether. A couple of years in a row, she wasn't there at all. When she was absent for months, she'd miss my birthday and not mention it, even when the first opportunity presented itself. Michelle and her mother didn't know when my birthday was, but my parents had already conditioned me to no longer care.

In the summer of my captivity, I turned twenty, though I could have turned fifteen or fifty or a hundred. Age became irrelevant. I walked into the large kitchen closet to look for a small cake. Maybe Corey thought of my birthday celebration. I looked through the shelves in the freezer, but I found nothing. Disappointed, I slammed the freezer door and walked outside.

The day was hot. I took off all my clothes, except for my undies, and sauntered into the swimming pool. My movement made small waves in the water, traveling on the surface. I walked until only my head was peeking from the water. The sun was beaming at me. I dunked my head in the water and stayed inside for as long as my breath allowed. All I could hear was the water in my ears.

On an early afternoon, as I spent another day at the pool, the gates noise startled me. I jumped up from the chair. My nerves rattled at the sight of the BMW parking on the cul-de-sac. I had seen nothing move or make sounds for a while.

I watched Corey get out of the car and face me. We waved at each other.

"Sam!"

I kept my hand in the air and waved. "Hello, Corey." My voice came out raspy from lack of use and my chest filled with warmth at the sight of him. Thank goodness he was back, and I wouldn't be alone again for a while. Even one day with him would lift my spirits.

"What have you done to yourself? You look as red as a lobster." I gazed down and couldn't tell the difference. I shrugged and got up to greet him. When I came closer, he gave me a strange look and said, "Is this all you've been up to? Sun tanning?"

"Yes. I'm sorry. I'm doing my best to find a job and move out."

He laughed. "Oh, no worries. Quite the opposite. I love having you here. Come."

He extended his arms, and I torpedoed toward him, landing in his warm hug. I missed a human touch.

We hugged for what seemed like forever. Before Corey released me, he landed a kiss on top of my head. "We should do something fun tonight. What do you think? Maybe dinner and movies?"

"Yes, that'd be fun!" Since my last venturing out into the world, I didn't dare walk far from the house again. I appreciated Corey's gesture to take me out into civilization.

He walked inside the house and looked around as if he was inspecting it.

"Boy, I miss my home when I travel." He said. He looked at me, and a layer of fog glazed over his eyes.

I half smiled and nodded. "I missed you, Corey."

"I'm going to rest up a bit, but I'll see you here around six."

"Sounds great."

Before six o'clock came, I took my time to get ready. After being in Corey's house all alone, a lot had happened and nothing happened at the same time. But one thing remained: I was still in search of myself and my new life here in L.A. It wasn't easy moving away from home and finding your way to success. It was especially difficult if, at the outset, there were no friends or acquittances or family members to help you move up. Hard work and luck were a winning combination. Hard work, I didn't mind. But luck —it was still on the trial period.

The bath helped relax me before I spent the evening with Corey. I was wondering what restaurant he'd take me to this time. What movie should we see? It was a great relief when I learned Corey liked movies like me. It was not surprising that he, a person of high caliber, knew people in the acting circles. Maybe luck was there, but it needed to be formed. It was in a caterpillar stage before it turned into a butterfly.

It had been a while since I'd put on makeup on. There wasn't any need to do so while all alone in the house. I wanted to look good for Corey, but also reinstate some sense of normalcy in my life. Given all that had happened in the last week, I needed it.

When I came downstairs a few minutes earlier than six, Corey was in the kitchen, cooking. He turned his head and looked at me over his shoulder. "Going somewhere?"

CHAPTER THIRTY-ONE

Surprise flicked through me at the sight of Corey cooking dinner in his kitchen.

"I thought we were going out tonight." I felt stupid for putting my makeup on and dressing up.

He turned around and looked at me up and down. He furrowed his brows and said, "I'm sorry. I should have made myself clearer, I guess. If you haven't noticed, I like to cook and there's nothing better than cooking for someone else."

"Oh. Well, in that case." I smiled. "Need any help?"

"No, I think I'm good." Corey seemed confident he could handle it all. "Do you want anything to drink?"

"How about..." I thought about my choice. "How about a glass of wine?"

"All right!" Corey seemed happy to hear me say that.

I didn't drink alcohol, but on rare occasions I did so. Talking to another human after many days called for such an occasion. Corey walked out of the pantry, carrying a bottle of red wine. He extended his arm and pointed the bottle at me. "Will this do?"

I knew nothing about wine except there were different colors.

"Hm. Yeah. That looks good." The label looked fancy enough.

He poured a glass of wine for both and he handed a glass to me. He walked to the stove and placed the food on the plates. The smell of fish and rice was making me hungry.

I sat down at the table, dizzy from the first sip of wine. A testament my body didn't handle alcohol well. Corey sat down, laying the plates on the table. He looked at me and furrowed his brows. "Are you okay?"

"Um. Yeah." I closed my eyes for a few seconds to recompose myself and grabbed the end of the table, afraid to lose balance.

"You look like you're about to pass out. Can I get you anything?"

"I'm good. Promise."

We ate in peace. The clattering of the forks and knives against the plates broke the awkward silence.

"So." I said. "I took a walk the other day and came across the small strip mall. It was super cute."

"Oh, the one on Main Street?"

"Yeah, I believe that's the one." I was still feeling woozy from the wine, but I did my best to carry on the conversation.

"What were you doing there?" His eyes widened in what looked like terror.

"I took a walk to clear my head a bit. Explore the neighborhood. The houses are amazing."

He swirled the wine in his glass. "Sure they are."

"I asked about a job in a small store, but it seems they already filled it. They should have taken the sign off the glass." I said. "Kind of misleading."

"That's a shame." Corey said and sipped his wine.

"Any word from Chris?"

He stood up from his chair and took his empty plate and mine half full. Corey didn't ask me if I was going to finish my dinner. He emptied my plate into the trash and placed the dishes inside the dishwasher. The sound of the plates clacking competed with his voice. "Not yet."

My heart sank. Corey looked at me, and I smiled to hide my agony.

"What do you think about nudging him?" I squeezed my hands hard under the table while maintaining my smile.

"No, no, no." Corey waved his hand. "In this business, you don't nudge people. It's a sure way to piss them off and get yourself on their permanent shit list."

"Okay." I said. "I don't want to sound impatient, and I appreciate your help, but I'm kind of at the end of my rope here. Frankly, I don't know how much longer I can wait."

"Sam, why rush? Life is ahead of you. Give yourself a break and enjoy. I'm sure Chris will return my text, and all you need to do is to be patient." His eyes on me were intent.

"Yes. Of course, I will try to be patient."

"Once we hear from Chris, your career will take off. Sit tight and wait. And be kind to your skin—it's looking borderline unhealthy."

An uproarious laugh came out of me. Corey took the bottle and poured more wine into both glasses.

"I think I saw you in your car near the strip mall the other day. I didn't know you were in town."

As soon those words, Corey lowered his shoulders and froze in place, giving me a stare as cold as ice. "Now, what makes you think that was me?"

I shrugged. "The white BMW. If it wasn't you, maybe it was your evil twin."

Another laugh came out, louder than the previous one. I grabbed my belly and kept laughing. Corey stared at me, waiting for the end of my hysteria.

"Is it possible that you were hallucinating?"

His question made me serious. I shook my head. "No."

I lied. Corey could not know about my psych ward episodes, and I was hoping he never would.

"No," I repeated. "It just seems like a coincidence that the person looked just like you and drove a white BMW."

Corey tilted his head to the side. "You think I'm the only one who drives a white BMW, Sam?"

"No, of course not," I rushed to answer. "Listen, let's forget about it. I must have missed you too much." I smiled, trying to regain his confidence in me. But Corey didn't smile back.

CHAPTER THIRTY-TWO

Corey took my hand and said, "Come."

"Where are you taking me?"

He didn't answer and pulled me toward the French door leading to the backyard. I shuffled behind him, trying to keep up with this pace. Where was he taking me? I squeezed his hand and told him to stop for a second so I could kick my stilettos and walk barefoot. He obliged and watched me struggle with taking the right one off.

He opened the front door where the starry night and a slight breeze awaited. Below us was the soft grass, a lush, dark green enveloped in the fresh night. Above us were the stars. So many of them.

Corey was looking up as if he was counting them.

"When I was a child, I thought the stars were a reflection of our eyes."

"Really?" I said.

"Yeah. And when it was cloudy and you couldn't see the stars in the sky, I believed an invisible layer of substance covered our eyes, hiding the reflection." He turned to me and looked at me for a long time. "I was relieved when I discovered the existence of stars had nothing to do with our eyes."

He moved toward me, squeezed my hand harder, and pulled me down to the grass. We laid there, looking above, wondering where the summer triangle was. It was the end of May and it might have just appeared in the Milky Way.

This was the Corey I enjoyed: kind and sensible. If I lived in the moment, he would now be a perfect guy, making me forget my true existence. Corey snuggled up to me and within seconds, he was kissing me passionately, with one hand caressing my hair. I opened my eyes, feeling lightheaded from the effects of alcohol. The stars swirled around and around until they disappeared. A black veil covered my eyes and my whole being disappeared into the night.

———

I woke up in my bed the following morning. The day was cloudy and gray, with potential rain to come. The house felt eerily quiet, like the calm before a storm. I attempted to listen to the sounds coming from the other parts of the house, but there was nothing. Where was Corey? I needed to ask him how I ended up in my bed. I couldn't recall anything from last night. The last thing I remembered was that Corey was kissing me on his lawn.

I looked to the side and noticed the dress I was wearing last night sat on the floor. Beneath the bed covers, my body was naked. I pulled up the cover to my chin, embarrassed by the sight. I looked around to see where my undergarments went, but nothing was in my proximity. It was time to face Corey and confront him about this. And while I was at it, it was time to ask all the questions I had meant to ask all along.

I stole out of the bed and grabbed a new pair of underwear. I slipped on a pair of jeans and a T-shirt and headed down to find Corey.

Fear and uncertainty gnawed at me as I walked down the stairs. A voice involuntarily came out of my mouth. "Corey." My own screaming voice startled me as it echoed between the walls. "Corey."

No response.

I entered the kitchen and walked a circle around the island. Maybe Corey left a note for me again, but I saw nothing. The kitchen looked different, but I couldn't tell what it was. Several objects were missing, but I never paid close enough attention to know which.

I screamed again, "Corey!"

Silence. The French door near the backyard was shut. I opened them and ran to the middle of the backyard, looking for Corey, but I didn't find him. It occurred to me to check if his BMW was still parked at the front. I ran and found nothing upon arrival. Corey had left without saying goodbye. He hadn't hung around to talk about what had happened between us last night. I thought it might have meant something to him when he kissed me passionately. He hadn't even let me know me how long he'd be away this time. Or where he was going to.

I felt a punch in my gut. Maybe Corey was an illusion last night. Was I losing my mind?

I couldn't remember much from last night. What happened to my memory? What was going on with me? I shook my head. This couldn't be real. And now, to learn that Corey would be gone for goodness knew how long was another reason to worry. Having no income, no job prospects, and no acting career in place, I felt doom looming in.

The walls closed in. I needed to get away from here before I lost what was left of my mind.

CHAPTER THIRTY-THREE

Two Months Later

When I woke up in my bed, Corey stood above me. His stature seemed larger than I remembered. His face looked inquisitive, like he was about to ask me something, but he bit his lower lip then smiled.

"Hi," he said. "It's time to get up."

"I'm tired," I said. "I can barely move."

"Oh, honey. I'm here if you need anything. I can only imagine how exhausted you might be." He caressed my hair and moved his hand to grab mine. "Only seven months left. It will fly by."

Seven months sounded like seven grueling decades. Especially since I hadn't seen my pregnancy coming at all.

Corey had arrived the day before from his trip. I hadn't seen him since his last appearance at the house. He made me take a pregnancy test to see the fruitful results of his courting. I did everything he'd asked of me, since Corey was the only person left to trust. When the test showed the positive result, I screamed. But that scream didn't manifest joy or happiness. It was a scream of horror.

While spending time alone, I had resorted deeper into my fear and ambivalence. Instead of venturing out to seek help, I'd stayed in the house and counted the days until a change in life happened. My phone had died since I could no longer make payments. One day, I strayed outside, hoping to reach the mall on a brisk walk. At the edge of the private path, upon seeing cars on the street, I placed my hands on my knees and screamed. The gravity pulled me toward the house and I turned around and ran and ran until I landed safely behind the gate.

The house was my private asylum, even though it contorted my mind.

Corey refused to talk about our love-making. When I told him I couldn't remember anything about it, he took offense to it.

"How do you not remember the special moments between us?"

I shrugged. "It could have been the wine."

I didn't remember making love to Corey, but it had to have happened. He didn't look surprised when he found out I was pregnant. He was beaming. I wanted to know what was next for Corey and me. Was he going to marry me now that I carried his child? Was I going to move to this house permanently and live a luxurious life, being a good wife and a mother? Corey was perhaps ready to settle down, but I had no desire to become a mother. I had set my career as a priority. The child would ruin it all.

Corey was here for only a couple of days before he left

for his trip. I didn't want him to go. Or better, I didn't want to stay alone. I needed to find a place, a hospital, that would help me get rid of my pregnancy. It wasn't too late. After all, Corey would understand. I was not his girlfriend or a wife prospect for a guy like him. I wasn't ready to put my career aside and prioritize my time and life to a child I didn't want.

Corey looked at me with concern in his eyes. "Is everything okay?"

I looked at the window, the opposite direction from Corey, and stared at it until I spoke up. "Listen, Corey." I gazed at him. He looked calm. "All of this... it all came too soon. Unexpectedly. I hope you would agree."

Corey's face expression remained the same. I wanted him to say something in return, but Corey nodded slowly, as if expecting me to go on.

His face expression was unnerving. When he looked at me like this, he didn't seem real or human. His face froze in time. It scared me to think what he was feeling at that moment, whether he would be agreeable to what I had to say, whether he wanted to admit all this was a terrible mistake and we would move on. I offered a smile, as if that would change everything. But Corey just stood there.

"Before it gets too late, I need to end this pregnancy. I'm wondering if you can take me to the hospital before you head out for another business trip."

Corey's eyes changed, like there was a fire lit inside them.

"That I cannot do," he said, his face expression motionless. "I'm afraid you won't get to decide on this baby's fate. I do."

Taken aback, I stared at Corey, hoping that all this was a bad dream and I'd wake up at any moment.

"I'm sorry. I don't understand what you're saying. We're not even a couple or married. You don't get to decide what I do with my body," I insisted. I was scared, but now was not the time to show my fear. Like sharks, people, too, would sense your fear and bite you.

"I'm afraid you're not in a position to decide, Sam. You're a big mess right now. You seem emotionally unstable, and I don't believe you can decide anything under these circumstances. So, since it's my child—I don't believe anyone else would qualify—I get to make a choice."

I succumbed to the dead silence. There was nothing to say. He could sense my vulnerability and weaknesses. He knew that turning into a brute would only make them pronounced. What did I get myself into? Who was Corey? Did he trap me with no way out of this terrible cycle?

"Now, get up and ready for the day. We're going for a long walk. It's good for you and the baby." Corey turned around and slammed the door behind him.

I had to run away as fast as possible. As soon as Corey left for his next trip, I'd find myself out of this forsaken place.

CHAPTER THIRTY-FOUR

The evening before he left for his next trip, I didn't see Corey at all. It hurt he didn't offer to make dinner like he had the previous times, although it didn't surprise me much. After our conversation about the baby the day before, our relationship turned cordial and strange. When I was in his proximity, he'd nod and walk by me. We didn't spend time together or have dinner. I no longer inquired about Chris, because we had a larger problem at hand now. If I didn't know Corey before, you could say he was a complete stranger now.

I peeked through the window of my room and noticed his car wasn't there. I roamed around the house like it was a jungle. The house, as usual, was quiet. I wondered where Corey had gone.

Feeling lost, I stormed into my room, ripped the clothes off the shelves, and shoved them into my suitcase. Everything I possessed—which was little to begin with—fit in one little bag. All my life was there. I had no place to go, no friends in town, no one to turn to, but my gut told me it was time to leave Corey's, even if that meant I would never get a chance to act. Once all my stuff was in the luggage, I turned around to see the room one last time and I cringed, reflecting upon the loneliness and silence I'd endured.

My luggage wasn't heavy at all. Like my life, it was almost empty. I just started heading for the door when Corey's car pulled into the driveway. When he saw me, he stormed out of the car and walked fast in my direction. My stomach churned, and as soon as he reached my side, he grabbed my luggage with all his might and said in a stern voice, "Where do you think you're going? Go inside!"

He held the suitcase in one hand while his other pointed at the front door. I stood there, unable to speak. Before I could compose my thoughts and say something, he grabbed my arm and pulled me inside. His powerful arms held a tight grip on mine. A bruise would emerge there soon enough. I wanted to scream, but no one in my proximity, except for Corey, would hear my voice.

Corey dragged me up the stairs and ushered me to my room. "Unpack your stuff right now. End of discussion."

He exited the room and his footsteps on the stairs echoed through the house. The door of my room was ajar; it was like a tease to freedom, but my decision to leave and escape was in vain. I sat down on the floor next to my luggage, cupped my face and sobbed. How could I have been so naïve and not seen any of this coming?

As a thought crossed my mind, I composed myself and wiped the tears with my hands. Corey was leaving tomorrow. He said he would be gone for a long trip. That promising thought put a smile on my face. I took the luggage, unpacked my clothes in haze, and went to bed to sleep off this terrible nightmare.

CHAPTER THIRTY-FIVE

I wasn't sure what time it was, but the emerging sunshine on the horizon suggested an early dawn when Corey walked into my room. He touched my shoulder and jerked it, pushing it toward the bed. Somberly, I gazed at him and expected yet another blow. He stood above me, smirking.

"Hey, Sam," he said. "I'm leaving now." He paused and stared at me as if he was looking for a reaction. "Don't do anything stupid. Okay? I will see you when I see you."

I stared back at him with my head still. As he stared back at me, I nodded, hoping he'd leave me alone. He bowed down and gave me a soft kiss on the cheek. "Take care, Sam. Be good to your child. I left prenatal vitamins in the kitchen for you to take. One a day is enough."

He smiled again like he was the most caring husband, not my absent roommate. I forced a smile back and said, "I will. Thank you."

Corey left, and I turned around to catch more sleep. Today was the day I'd escape. Neither this house nor Corey would ever see me again.

When I woke up, it was almost noon. I had to keep reminding myself I was carrying a baby, and that pregnancy was making me sloth-like and tired. But I'd reserved enough energy to walk as many miles as needed until I found a safe place. It was true—I had no money, no savings, not even a cellphone to call my mother to pick me up, but the survival mode would find its way to victory. I had faith something would come along on my lonely journey.

I went downstairs to grab some food and water for my escape exit. When I arrived in the kitchen, I saw the box of prenatal vitamins Corey had mentioned sitting on the kitchen island. I took it in my hand, joggled it, and threw it in the trash. The food closet's door was wide open, and I rushed in and grabbed whatever was closest to my hands. A few bottles of water would quench the thirst during my trip. I stopped and sighed. This nightmare would be over soon.

With a handful of food, I returned to my room and packed it in my luggage. I didn't even look back to see if anything of mine was still there. Freedom was the only thing on my mind, and I couldn't wait to embrace it.

Part of me felt like someone was watching me. As I walked across the living room, I thought I heard steps behind me. Shivers travelled down my spine. When I turned around, the air was clear. I continued walking into freedom with a sense of relief. The front door opened to a day that was drenched in sunshine. It was as if a heaven awaited on the other side after a hard life.

As I approached the gate, I repeated the code in my head: 1115. 1115. 1115. My mind was good at storing numbers into my memory. As I brought my hands to the lock, they were shaking. I grabbed the lock and with measured moves, I slowly typed in the numbers. 1. 1. 1. 5. The red flashing light came on. In my agitation, was it possible I typed the numbers too fast? I repeated the exercise, but the red light flashed again and the gate appeared solidly motionless. Again and again, I tried to no avail.

Corey must have changed the code. A punch in the stomach told me that immediately. He'd trapped me there. I had nowhere to go. I looked up at the gate, and the height was trice mine. There was no way I could climb it up, especially since there were no perpendicular bars to rest my foot on to advance up. But maybe there was another exit somewhere in the house's proximity. There had to be.

In panic, I ran along the fence to find an alternative exit. There had to be a hole, a narrow path out. The high hedges against the fence didn't allow me to see the other side well. I'd stop at one spot and look through the hedges to see if there was any space without the fence. As I explored more, it looked less and less promising. After I'd searched the entire perimeter with no luck, my heart sank.

I dragged across the lawn, and in the middle of it, I fell to the ground. Above me was the perfect blue sky. In such vastness, my world now revolved around captivity. A scream came out of my mouth. And another. Then another. But no one was around me to hear my voice of incredible pain and agony.

CHAPTER THIRTY-SIX

I didn't eat or do much for days. Time became irrelevant. I'd curl up and stare at a spot wherever my body anchored for the day. I no longer wanted to feel or live. I'd rock myself to sleep and wake up to start the same process all over again.

One evening, someone knocked on my bedroom window, filling my whole body with terror. Heart pounding, I sat up on the bed and drew the covers to my face. My bedroom was on the second floor, with no access to the window from the outside. Who or what could it be? I waited for a few seconds to investigate in case the knocking repeated, and just as I approached the window, the knocking happened again.

My heart ramped up even further. I feared whatever was outside. Part of me didn't want to know. Darkness had already enveloped the house, and it was difficult to see anything. I inched closer to the window gingerly, my fists clenched in sweat. As I came nearer, a voice behind me startled me. "Sam."

I screamed.

When I turned around, my father was sitting at the edge of the bed. He looked at me and smiled. The day of the accident, he wore the same shirt and pants. He looked youthful and healthy. Almost even happy. It was good to see him smile again.

"Dad, what are you doing here?" I was happy to see him, but he should have announced his visit. I didn't like surprises.

"Delightful house." He looked around and nodded his head in approval. "I wanted to stop by and visit. It's been a long time."

"How did you find me?"

"I didn't need to look too hard," he said. "Have you spoken to Mother?"

"I... I haven't, no. What day is it?" I looked around, searching for an answer.

My father put a finger on his mouth and said. "Hm. You don't know what day it is? That's troubling, Sam."

"What do you want, Dad?" I stiffened my tone. I dreaded the question, but I had to ask.

"Nothing. I heard you were here and wanted to check up on you, see how you're doing."

"Well, things are okay. They could be better, for sure." I paused for a second and considered whether I should tell him the whole truth. Dad and I had never had a relationship as adults, so I wasn't sure how receptive he would be to me opening up to him. I hadn't spoken to anyone other than Corey for months. I yearned for company. I was desperate to be heard and be helped. My stubbornness could be kept at bay for any little help I could get.

I told my dad the truth. "Dad, I'm trapped here. I have

no way to go. Corey locked me in here, but I don't under-stand why."

I lowered my gaze in embarrassment that I let it all happen.

"Listen," he said. "None of it is your fault. I have good news for you, though."

He smiled at me and lifted his index finger in the air. "There's a way out of here. If you follow me, I will lead you to your freedom."

"There is?" I was surprised to hear it. The day I real-ized I was locked in, I checked every nook and cranny and I had found no way out.

He nodded. "And you know what? It's not that difficult at all."

Relieved to hear this, I ran to the closet and grabbed my luggage, intact, waiting for me to take it when the opportunity to escape presented itself.

"I'm ready," I announced, holding my luggage.

Dad got up from the bed and walked toward the door. He turned around to find my eyes filled with hope, despair, and ambiguity all at once. He'd make sure I followed him. My father moved without turning back. He seemed so comfortable in this house, as if he had been here many times before. He knew where to go, and I followed him down the stairs and out of the front door before heading to the gate.

When we hit the front yard, I called for my father. "Dad, wait." He turned around and looked at me, concerned that something might have happened. "Dad, do you have the gate code? How are we going to leave the place? Where did you get the code from?"

"Just follow me." His voice was shaking and soft.

He continued walking, and I quickened my steps to catch up to him. When I walked a few more steps, I tripped and fell on the ground. My face burrowed into the grass. I felt pain on my left hip. Father refused to stop, even though he'd heard me yelp. My eyes squinted in pain. When I opened them, I turned to my left to glimpse my father; he was already at a fair distance from me. He kept walking until I could see nothing but the trees' shadows.

"Dad!" I yelled. "Dad!"

He didn't respond. "Dad, I'm sorry. I'm so sorry, Dad. Please forgive me. I love you, Dad. Please. Please. Get me out of here. Please."

I sobbed until the tears lulled me into a solid sleep.

CHAPTER THIRTY-SEVEN

Birds in a small cluster flew above me and gawked loudly. My right eye opened before the left one did until the entire sky appeared in front of me. I was still lying on the lawn, curled up. I stood up with great difficulty and propped myself with my right arm. My hair was in complete disarray. I licked the edges of my lips and tasted salt from dried tears on my face. In front of me stood the locked gate I wanted to escape through, and on the other side stood the house. I wanted to burn it down.

The pain throbbed down my legs and my arms. I looked down at my knees and noticed the bloody marks. I couldn't remember what happened or how I fell. The memory of how I ended up on the lawn escaped me. Did I try another failed attempt to escape? My luggage lied next to me as a sign.

I reluctantly entered the house and walked to the pantry to get a bottle of water. Hunger came and left, but my mouth was still too dry. I gobbled down the water and felt the energy shoot up my veins like electricity.

Still in pain, I lay on the couch to compose my thoughts. I had long denied my pregnancy, but it was all too real. The unwanted child inside me was making me tired all the time. I hated feeling tired. Despite being a prisoner to Corey's idea, I still wanted to pursue acting and be on the world stage. There was nothing better than pretending to be someone else and feeling someone else's fears and desires. Corey had cut the cord with my chance to succeed, but the world wasn't over yet.

I stood up quickly from the couch with renewed energy. It was time to search for a metal coat hanger. Michelle once told me that her grandmother used it to get rid of an unwanted pregnancy. Lots of women used it back when abortion was taboo or illegal. It wasn't safe by any means, but it would achieve a desired outcome: the unwanted child would no longer be attached to me.

I ran to my room and frantically opened up the closet doors. In anticipation of seeing the coat hangers hanging from the rack, my heart sank when I realized nothing was there. Absolutely nothing. I scoffed and exited my room, running to the room next to mine. I opened up the closet there, and the same—empty and void of any objects.

It wasn't so extraordinary that no coat hangers were provided in guest rooms. It occurred to me that the primary bedroom, Corey's room, had to have them. What young professional wouldn't have this essential item for suits and shirts?

His bedroom was on the main floor. Though I'd lived in this house for months, I had not seen his room yet. Walking in for the first time felt like a crime. Breaking and entering. When I let the door swing ajar, I peeked in to check if the air was clear. Corey's room looked nothing as

I pictured it. I'd imagined some masculinity as the first word describing his room, except for the pink walls and satin sheets covering the bed. I looked around to get any clues what Corey was like, but there was nothing to produce a story.

The closet was already wide open. Corey must have been in a rush the morning he left the room. It took a second to realize the strangeness of the sight in front of me: the closet was completely empty. There were no shirts or suits hanging. Where did Corey keep his clothes? Most disappointingly, there were no coat hangers anywhere.

I came to the dresser across from his bed, opening every drawer like a lunatic and finding that each one was completely empty. I didn't understand how Corey lived. Shirtless and suit-less. None of this made any sense.

Lost and confused, I ran to the kitchen to look for a knife or any other sharp object. Corey must have removed all the knives, because the countertops were all empty. Now I realized why the kitchen looked so different—it was stripped of any object I could use to hurt myself or my baby.

Beaten down by this discovery, I put my elbows on the kitchen island and buried my face in my hands. What was my next move? I forced myself to think.

CHAPTER THIRTY-EIGHT

I was lying in my bed, staring at the ceiling. It was an early morning, or so I thought. I wasn't ready to face the day yet. The ceiling became dizzying, so I closed my eyes. A childhood tune vibrated between my lips. It was a song my mother used to sing to me when I was a happy child. Her voice was soothing and beautiful. I'd fight sleep so I could keep listening. She'd stroke my hair until I fell asleep. When I finished the song, I came to dead silence. And then it happened. It happened suddenly like a death by a lightening. The voices in my head returned.

They didn't scream; they whispered. I tried to discern them and see if I recognized them. Perhaps my father was calling me to let me know of his imminent return. But the voice I distinctly heard was a woman.

"Michelle, is it you?" I said.

She called my name again, and I didn't think I knew her voice. It was stern and alarming and it was trying to tell me something. I squinted my eyes to hush the voice away, but the whisper was becoming a clear and loud sound.

"You deserve this. You made choices that led you to this. And now, sinful and remorseless, this is the price you pay for. Your child is only going to suffer. May God save the child. May God bless the child. You should have known better. Now burn!"

"No!" I screamed from the top of my lungs. "No, no, no!"

I clenched my fists and opened my eyes, blinded by the brightness entering through the window. Outside my door, I heard quick steps moving away from me, like they were about to go down the stairs.

"Who is it? Show yourself!" I screamed. The voice prodded and haunted me. "Corey? Corey, is it you? Corey!"

My call remained unanswered. When would Corey return? I needed to tell him all this was a terrible mistake. He needed to let me go, or karma would catch up to him, eventually.

I lost count of the time. It could have been a few days since Corey left or a whole week, maybe even a couple. I couldn't even guess.

It was much too early, but I thought I felt a few kicks from the inside. The child was trying to communicate. What do you want, you annoying pest? I called the human inside me 'it', for I couldn't even guess if it was a boy or a girl. It was an unwelcome intruder in my body and life. Its kicks were gentle enough to show weakness and early age, but strong enough to invoke a protest and rage inside me. I needed to discard it before it was too late.

But the voices in my head hated me.

I didn't get out of bed all day. By the time evening

came, the hunger was unbearable. My body was weak and brittle. I held onto the stairway railing to avoid a fall. When I arrived at the kitchen, I eagerly opened the food closet and grabbed whatever was closest to my hands. It was a small apple, and I bit into it, the crunching sound echoing in my ears. The apple was delicious. I was at least fortunate to have all this food available to me.

My head was clearing. I sighed and lifted my arm to see if my hand was still shaking. It seemed steadier, like my mind.

I looked through the kitchen French door into the backyard and noticed something different about it. A chair that was sitting next to the table now stood in front of the door. I couldn't remember moving it, but that was impossible. Being alone and lonely in this house for months, I could remember every move of mine and every thought that crossed my mind. Loneliness made my senses pronounced.

I was sure I didn't do it.

When I opened the French door, the heat splashed me immediately. It wasn't just any kind of heat; it was an oppressive kind that would make you regret being outside for even a minute. There were visible marks on the floor, as if someone dragged the chair. I kneeled down to touch and inspect them and, through my amateur analysis, the marks were still fresh. I looked to my right, then left, but there was nobody in sight. Not even birds who must have been finding a reprieve from the heat.

It was entirely possible my mind was tricking me again, but I felt lucid. I went back to the food closet and grabbed a bottle of water, downing it in one slurp. Breathless, I gasped for air, my diaphragm moving fast under my chin.

Slowly moving back to my room, I resolved to do something fun today—maybe go to the pool and get some suntan. Or watch a movie, my once-upon-a-time favorite activity. Or maybe I'd look for a notebook and a pen and start jotting down my thoughts and feelings. Someone told me once it was an activity for someone in distress. The sky was the limit.

As I walked down the hallway to my room, a strange feeling came over me, as if someone was watching me. But that wasn't that. In the corner of my eye, I noticed something different about the second floor. When I came closer to my room, the room that had been locked was open. I had attempted to open this door before, with no luck. But now—the door was ajar and looked welcoming.

I put my hand on the doorknob and twisted it. The room was pitch-black. I looked for the light switch on the wall and flipped it.

CHAPTER THIRTY-NINE

Wide-eyed, I looked to my left, then right, when I entered the room. It was empty. I'd expected to see an electric chair or torture chamber, but none of that was there. Instead, the room looked quite ordinary, like it was someone's office. There was a desk and a chair on one of side of the room, and on the other, a smaller couch for visitors. The walls were painted greenish, a calming hue for the eye. The blinds made the room pitch-dark. Like in the rest of the rooms, the long bay windows featured silk white curtains. What was there to hide?

There was nothing extraordinary in the room until a wall on the same side of the door drew my attention. I came closer to examine the collage of baby photos hung on the wall.

"What... what is this?" I whispered to myself. Each picture had a baby up to a year-old. None seemed to be older than one. I scanned through their faces, and all of them looked sad with strange, droopy eyes. I touched one picture and tilted my head, examining the baby. Where was she now? Who was she? Why was her picture plastered on the wall like in a museum?

I walked a step back and looked at all of them individually, noticing one common theme among them. They all had big blue eyes and blonde hair. Were they siblings? Born to the same mother? Or perhaps the same father? So many questions lingered in my mind until an unfamiliar voice disrupted my train of thoughts. "What are you doing in here?"

I screamed and put my hands around my torso in self-defense. In front of me stood a woman in her forties—that was my guess—with a stern and robotic look. She was lean and muscular for her age, looking disproportionate with her gray hair on top. She stared at me with a hard look, as if she had knives in her eyes that were about to stab me.

"Who, who are you?" I stammered.

"You should not be in this room. Out." She pointed her index finger to the hallway and ushered me outside. As I stood in the hallway, she closed the room and locked it behind.

"Are you going to answer my question?" I followed her as she stormed down the stairs. "Hey! Hey, talk to me! How did you get inside?"

When we came down the stairs, she settled on a kitchen stool and looked at me with the same robotic look.

"My name is Shauna. I'm here to take care of you."

"Take care of me? What's that supposed to mean?"

"Corey asked me to live here while you carry the baby and take care of you."

"Corey? Where is he? When is he coming home?"

She kept looking at me with no intention of providing

an answer. I lifted my arm and pointed at the backyard. "How did you get in?"

"Without a problem."

"Did Corey give you the code for the gate? What is it? What is it?" I screamed.

"Calm down." She raised her voice. "You're hysterical." She made a disgusted face. "And you look awful. When was the last time you took a shower?"

I ignored her question. I couldn't remember the last time.

"Was it you who moved that chair outside? Was it?" My voice was surprisingly confident.

Shauna nodded once.

"When did you get here? I didn't hear you when you entered the house."

"This morning. You were still sleeping."

I looked at her with suspicion. "Okay, well. Tell Corey I don't need anyone to take care of me."

"Unfortunately, that's not happening." She stood up from the stool and walked to the guest room. "Corey wanted me to ensure that you receive the best possible care while you're carrying his child." She said the word child with force and determination.

I shook my head. "I've already told Corey this baby is a mistake. Take me to the hospital and help me get rid of it, for God's sakes!"

Shauna laughed. "You're crazy if you think that will happen. Now, go take a bath. It will be good for you." She took a magazine from the coffee table and flipped through the pages. Shauna sat on the couch, as if she just were my long-lost cousin who'd come for a visit over a weekend. If I had to guess, given her demeanor, Shauna was bullied a lot in school.

Though, I had to admit that part of me didn't mind her being around. After not talking to another human being for months, she was a welcome reprieve, although I knew we would never become friends.

Maybe Shauna had answers to my questions. She might finally untangle the knot that my life had become.

CHAPTER FORTY

Mostly, Shauna and I cohabited in peace. Even though it was just the two of us, the house seemed livelier. She dusted off the CD player in the main foyer and played music every day. Frank Sinatra was her favorite, but when she was in a good mood, for whatever reason, she'd play AC/DC or Soundgarden. We left each other alone unless Shauna had to take care of me and complete daily tasks.

She came to my room early in the morning and hand me a pill and a glass of water.

"Take it," she said. A large red pill sat on her extended palm, and I assumed it was prenatal. Did she fish them out of the trash? That would be gross. I took the pill from her hand and swallowed it, gulping the water quickly. I'd collapsed in bed and she would exit my room, slamming the door behind her. Every single time.

Shauna didn't make a reappearance until noon, when she carefully prepared my meal. It usually comprised vegetables and protein. She yelled out my name from the guest room and told me I had five minutes to get out, or else she'd come get me.

One day, she sat across from me, her arms on the table, and watched me play with my food. I didn't feel hungry. She'd fed me eggs in the morning with yogurt and fruit and they'd fill me up for hours.

"Eat. You must eat. That baby needs to be fed."

I lifted my head from my plate and gave Shauna a smile. "Shauna. Please admit that you don't want to be here. Do you?" I squinted my eyes and gave her a sharp look I didn't think she was expecting. She wiggled in her chair as if she was uncomfortable and mumbled something.

"What did you say?" I asked.

"I said, I am on my duty and don't mind being here. It's a beautiful house."

I laughed. She didn't appreciate the uproar. I made a serious face to put her at ease and continued, "How do you and Corey know each other?"

"Why should it matter?"

"Oh, it doesn't, really. I'm just curious. You know, I really miss Corey. When is he coming back exactly? I've been here... like, forever, and I honestly can't tell what day is today."

"Corey will come when he wants to. I don't have access to his schedule and we don't talk every day."

"I see. And... I really want to know." I leaned forward and grimaced. "Why exactly am I being held captive here?"

Her eyes widened in surprise. "Corey didn't tell you?"

"Tell me what?"

"Hm," she said in a nonchalant tone. "I guess you'll just have to wait and hear from him."

"Hear what? Is there a reason you can't tell me?"

"Absolutely not. It's none of my business what you two come up with. My only job is to care for your baby." She stood up from her chair and poured a glass of water in the kitchen sink. She turned toward me and said, "We're having a visitor tomorrow. A nurse practitioner to check up on your baby."

"What? That is ridiculous," I protested.

"What exactly is ridiculous about it?"

"Why can't we go to the hospital like all other normal people?"

She grinned. "Corey will be here soon enough. He will explain."

With that statement, she turned around and walked away. My eyes followed her as she turned around the corner. In a muffled sound, I heard her voice. "And eat the damn food!"

CHAPTER FORTY-ONE

I longed for the day Corey would arrive home and explain what was going on. The anticipation was killing me. I'd been racking through my brain about what I could do to escape, but nothing clever was coming to mind. It was almost as if someone had already conditioned me to be a prisoner. A prisoner who deserved to be one. For a crime. A murder. A manslaughter. It was all coming together like karma knocking on my door.

Fear haunted me, though I tried to hide it. I was an actress, after all.

The following day, I saw Shauna sunbathing outside. She wore a pair of shorts, a tank top, and a visor. Her long legs dangled over the edge of the recliner. Her hands gripped the sides, and she barely moved. I opened the French door slowly to not startle her, but she flinched and sat upright, regardless. She turned around and looked at me as if wondering what I wanted from her.

"May I sit here?" A chair was nearby, and I sat down even though Shauna didn't respond.

She laid back and turned her head slightly in the opposite direction from me. I couldn't tell if my presence annoyed her, but I didn't care. It was then I observed Shauna a little better. Her skin looked like someone poured bleach all over her. A blue tattoo of a soldier and a helicopter flying above covered her entire shin. I wondered if she was a soldier herself.

As my eyes moved up her body, I noticed a wound on her left thigh, slightly covered by her shorts. That explained why Shauna walked unevenly.

"Hey, Shauna," I whispered. "Were you ever in a war battle?"

I stared at her, looking for an answer, but she remained silent. When I turned my head to look straight ahead, she said, "Yes."

"Which war?"

"Iraq. But I don't want to talk about it now. Or ever." She adjusted her head against the chair pillow and pulled her visor lower on her face.

I leaned against the chair and absorbed the heat. Minutes had passed when we found comfort in our surroundings. I asked her, "Hey, Shauna. I need to ask you another question."

She turned around and looked at me. Her face was expressionless. She seemed unbothered by my presence, which surprised me, given she had avoided me in the house. I felt she wanted to be alone all the time and didn't want to mingle, but perhaps she, too, needed company once in a while. "Yeah, shoot."

"Do you think you can drive me somewhere, maybe today or tomorrow?" I wanted to go visit Spy Café and find Michael. Ask for his help. Find a phone and call my mother secretly.

She stared at me for a second and turned her head back. "No."

I rolled my eyes and was thankful she didn't see me.

"Well, how about I take myself? Maybe you will let me borrow your car."

She laughed. "Oh, dear. Do you really think I'd be that stupid to let you get away?" She waved her left hand at me and said, "That would be a hard pass."

My shoulders slumped in this hopeless conversation. "How about you let me walk around the neighborhood? You can come with me. I just... I just yearn for the outside world. I'm kinda sick of this house." I looked up at the window where the bird had once ended its life. "I... I just need to feel a little normalcy once again."

She looked at me and shook her head. "Sorry."

I leaned against the chair and stared at the hedges in front of me. I longed for things that were on the other side. There was a long street that led to a strip mall. There were people walking on the sidewalk, walking their dogs, saying hello to each other. Or not. It didn't matter. They were free to do whatever they desired. Free. I yearned for my freedom. For Michelle. She had to be worried sick about me. Maybe she'd already began the search process with the police. Maybe someone would eventually find me here and rescue me.

I was trying to think about what traces I'd left to help anyone find me, but my move to the house was unexpected, so there were none.

"Shauna." I began. "I don't even know how I got pregnant. I mean, yes, I had to be intimate with Corey, but I remember nothing about it. Not even a glimpse."

Shauna adjusted her visor and slumped in the chair. "And?"

"Don't you think that's strange? I mean, how did Corey get me pregnant in the first place?"

"You're asking me?"

"It's a rhetorical question. I just don't remember my memory being so bad." Shauna looked at me, and we both laughed.

"There goes your answer," she said.

"Seriously. It concerns me. But... I can't help but think that he drugged me to have sex with me."

"Listen. I really don't want to get into your intimate life with Corey or anyone else. I'm here for one reason only." Her voice sounded defensive and angry. "A nurse is coming over this evening. Be ready."

She stood up from the chair and stormed through the door.

CHAPTER FORTY-TWO

At exactly seven in the evening, the front gate opened up and a black Mercedes drove through. It parked behind Shauna's car. I stood at the window of my room and fantasized about walking through the gate or entering the car and driving off with a mad speed. The gate closed behind the car and the dust from the path settled. A woman in her thirties approached the front door and seconds later, she rang the doorbell. The closed door of my room muffled Shauna's voice. I couldn't tell what she was saying to the woman who had just arrived.

The voices were getting closer, but I still couldn't tell what they were saying. I sat on the edge of my bed, anticipating their arrival—that was what they were here for. My child. I stared at one spot. I didn't want to be caught doing anything else, and as the door opened, I looked up to see the two women standing at the door.

"Here's she is," Shauna announced. She looked at me with twinkly eyes and added a smile to her face. It was the first time I saw Shauna smile. People looked a lot more trusting when carrying a smile. The woman stood next to her, mouth wide open.

"Wow, she is a beauty."

She herself was pampered with long, silky blonde hair, beautiful blue eyes, the subtle makeup highlighting her features. She wore a short black dress and over her shoulder was a large bag.

"Thank you," I said and then felt stupid for it.

They stepped inside the room, and Shauna went immediately towards the windows to close the blinds. I did a double take, not understanding what she was hiding us from. I didn't ask questions.

The other woman stood next to me and extended her arm. "Hi. I'm Leslie. I'll be checking up on your baby today." Her voice was high pitched, like she was happy about this visit and everyone else would be, too.

I extended my arm back and grabbed hers limply. "I'm Sam."

"Sam. That's a beautiful name." She put the bag on the bed and took a device out and some other tools I hadn't seen before. When she saw me looking at her with furrowed eyes, she laughed and said, "Oh, don't worry, this is just a Doppler, which is something we use to monitor the baby's heart. We're going to listen to the baby's heart."

She ordered me to lie down and, as if I was hypnotized, I did as she asked. Shauna stood next to the window and watched us from there with her arms crossed. Her smile had disappeared and her look was razor sharp. Her shadow moved on the blinds behind her.

Leslie instructed me to pull up my T-shirt and lower my underwear. She slowly put warm jelly on my abdomen and gazed at me once in a while. "This won't hurt, sweetheart."

Leslie placed a belt around me and moved the ultra-sound transducer all around my belly until she settled for one spot. She pressed the transducer lightly and watched the small monitor hooked up to the ultrasound. She reached for the volume button and, like a train in high speed coming your way, I heard it. I heard the little heart-beat of my unborn child.

Leslie smiled and turned to me. "Do you hear it?"

But the room swirled around and around and, even if I tried hard, I could not have kept my conscious. I could still hear the life inside me, even though the room was dark. The terror. The beauty. The demise.

Next, I felt wet hands slapping my face. Leslie screamed above me, trying to bring me back. "Sam, Sam. Are you okay?"

Her image was blurry. Shauna stood next to her. Her silhouette was by now recognizable. Tough and unloving. Leslie turned to her and asked her to bring a glass of water. Shauna left the room, and I mustered the strength to whisper.

"I... I need help."

"What?" Leslie's voice sounded grave and concerned. "What did you say?"

"I need help. I need to get out of here."

But just as Leslie grasped my last words by squeezing my hand tight, Shauna walked into the room carrying a glass of water. She was swift. Leslie propped me on the bed and handed me the glass.

"You need to rest up, sweetheart." Her voice was

gentle. "Your baby seems to be perfectly fine. But you need to take care."

Shauna nodded once in agreement and, once Leslie packed up the instruments in silence, the two of them exited my room without saying a word. Once again, I heard muffled voices. The women were carrying a full-on conversation. What were they saying?

Soon enough, I'd find out. And then I'd regretted trusting the smiling face.

CHAPTER FORTY-THREE

"How are you feeling?" Shauna probed when she saw me in the kitchen the following morning.

"Fine," I said.

"Good."

She was preparing breakfast for me and my child.

"Is it eggs again today?" I inquired. She ignored my question.

"I had an interesting conversation with Leslie yesterday," Shauna proceeded. "Leslie tells me you wanted her to help you escape." She turned around, holding a large knife as if she was about to strike. I remained silent. "Unfortunately for you, Leslie will not help you. Anyone who crosses the threshold of this house can never help you. You can only dream of that."

"Hm. I don't recall asking Leslie for help." I said. "I was unconscious and didn't know what the heck was going on."

"Leslie was certain about what she heard. Why would I not believe her?"

I lifted my arms up and waved them. "I think Leslie is full of shit."

"Excuse me? Leslie would have no reason to lie. I've known her for over ten years, and she just met you."

I smiled. "Oh, Shauna. Don't believe everything you hear. I have no intention of escaping. This house is delightful." My eyes were looking around. "It's a beautiful place. And you're taking care of me. What else would I want?"

She looked at me, studying me up and down. She tilted her head like she didn't believe me and yelled out, "Since when?"

"I see how you might disbelieve me. I mean, one day, I press you for answers about my captivity, the next, I tell you I'm happy here. Sure, anyone in their right mind would question my sanity at the least. But I assure you, I have no intention of escaping. I'm fine, because, you know why, Shauna?" She squinted her eyes at me and awaited. "You know why?"

"Why?"

"Because I have no place to go! I'm penniless, I have no friends or family here, not a soul to take care of me, and I'm pregnant. What are my options in the world outside?" I smirked. "So, tell me. Do you believe me now?"

She stared at me, surprised at my monologue. "Whether or not you're lying, it doesn't matter. You're not going anywhere, and I am here to make sure that happens."

"I'll make your job easy, Shauna. Don't you worry." I said. Shauna turned around and bustled things around, continuing to make breakfast.

I sat at the table and waited for her to serve me the

food. The smell of eggs was wafting through the air. I couldn't tell her I was sick of them, but I had enough resolve to pretend they were the best eggs I had ever had.

I watched her place the eggs on the plate and add a slice of wheat bread next to it. She walked fast toward me and, without looking at me, she put the plate on the table in front of me and walked away.

"What about you? Are you going to eat something?" I took the fork and stabbed the eggs with it.

"No. I eat early."

I crinkled up my nose and move the eggs to the side of the plate. Shauna walked out of the kitchen, and I jumped out of my chair to grab myself a cup of water. Shauna didn't allow me to do anything around the house for one obvious reason: I was pregnant and I wasn't supposed to strain myself. It wouldn't bother me so much if even the simplest task wasn't a strain at all.

I opened up a kitchen cabinet above the sink where I'd find a glass. Corey supplied all glasses made of plastic, none out of the glass, to ensure extra safety. At the forefront, there was an orange pill box. Curious to find out what it was, I grabbed it to read the label.

UNISON, Sleep Aid

What were the sleeping pills doing in the kitchen? Like a slap on the face, I realized Corey had to use them to put me to sleep and take advantage of me. I ran to the first bathroom, kneeled on the floor next to the toilet, and threw up.

CHAPTER FORTY-FOUR

Things started to make sense. Corey drugged me twice with the pills in the kitchen. He must have crushed pills into powder and put it in my food or drink he'd been so eager to share with me.

If my assumption was true, I didn't understand Corey's motive of getting me pregnant without my consent. The last time I'd heard of something like this was when a local woman in New Mexico met a man in a bar who bought her a drink and slipped her something to make her fall asleep at the wheel on her way back home. When the cops found her several hundred feet off the road, they pronounced her dead.

The news made it to our little town, and everyone panicked. Our town in New Mexico had been low in crime, an occasional break-in for a petty theft, but other than that, we all felt safe. They had caught the man who caused the woman's death and when he came on trial; he confessed he had wanted her dead, because she'd rejected his advances several times and refused to go on a date with him.

I recalled the snippets of his trial in the news. My mother and I had sat in front of the TV and watched the proceedings. The man looked quite handsome and, if you looked at him, you'd never suspect that the person could commit such a horrendous crime. But those were the worst. They were wolves disguised in a sheep's coat.

My mother had turned her head toward me and watched me. "Sam," she'd said. "You never accept a drink from a stranger. Do you understand?"

"Mom!" I said. "I'm barely nineteen. I'm legally not allowed to drink."

She nodded twice and returned to watching the news.

It didn't matter what parents say or what advice they give. The child will do what their instinct told them was right. For all I knew, moving into Corey's house would solve all my worries.

Shauna knocked on my door and disrupted my train of thoughts.

"Yes?" I said.

She opened the door and announced, "Corey will be here soon. He will want to talk to you."

"Okay." I said. "Is there anything I should do to prepare myself?" My heart dropped into my stomach at the thought of being in the same room as him.

"Prepare? No. All you need to do is listen." She stepped outside the room and slammed the door behind her. I got up and followed her.

"Hey, Shauna." We both stood in the hallway, facing each other. "Thank you for letting me know. I look forward to seeing Corey."

She looked me up and down, and with slight suspicion, said, "Okay. I guess I'm glad to hear that."

She turned around and walked down the stairs. I watched her at the top of the stairs, holding onto the railing. I watched the top of her head moving like a pawn on a chessboard.

When I returned to my room, I took off all my clothes. I entered the bathroom and stood against the mirror to check out my profile. A little bump formed on my stomach just enough to show a life inside me. The rest of me was all skin and bones from days of ignoring hunger. My eyes had sunk deeper into my socket and my hair showed a couple of inches of brown roots. The rest of my dyed blonde hair covered my back.

I tilted my head and stared at myself. "Oh, wow." I smiled. I cupped my hands on my stomach and stroked it in a clockwise motion. I giggled. "How amazing." My voice was soft and in awe of the sight. What would Corey say when he saw me? What kind of father would he be?

I furrowed my brow to abate these thoughts. What was happening to me? I should be terrified and furious, but my emotions kept zipping from one place to another. I started running water in the bathtub, eager to get some relaxation. There was nothing like a warm bath to relieve stress.

When I got comfortable in the bathtub, I closed my eyes and listened to the sound of the water waves forming with my movements. The coziness and warmth were lulling me to sleep. A few minutes must have passed when a voice came out of nowhere.

"Sam?"

"Oh my God!" I screamed.

My father stood above the bathtub and watched me with his gigantic eyes. He looked angry and I could tell there was something on his mind that he wanted to get out.

"Sam, why are you still here?"

"Dad! We tried to escape together, but you disappeared on me. Why did you leave me like that?"

He moved his head to the right and said, "Sam. This is not about me, darling. You need to take charge of your life."

"But, Dad." I curled up beneath the bath bubbles, feeling ashamed.

"Ah. Ah. Ah. Don't 'but, Dad' me. You got yourself into this mess. You need to get yourself out of it."

"Dad!"

"I'm telling you, Sam." He raised his voice. "You need to get yourself out of this."

"Please, Dad!"

"Sam! Repeat after me: 'I need to get myself out of this'."

"Daaaad!"

I squeezed my eyes as hard as possible and clenched both my fists. I didn't realize I was screaming from the top of my lungs until Shauna stormed through the door. "What is going on here?" She grabbed my shoulders and shook me. "Sam, what is going on? Who were you talking to?"

My stare remained trained on the small bubbles on the water's surface, and I could feel my heart pounding.

Shauna looked around to examine the bathroom, but there was nothing but a misty air around us. She released a breath and made a matter-of-fact statement. "Corey is here. Come down as soon as you're ready."

CHAPTER FORTY-FIVE

When I came out of the bath, I put on a pair of shorts and a T-shirt—the only clothes that fit me well. I'd asked Shauna if she could take me shopping for maternity clothes, but, of course, as always, she'd shut me down right away and told me she would go shopping herself. I was still waiting.

I debated whether to put makeup on to brighten my face a bit, but decided against it. Instead, I put my hair in a high ponytail. I smacked my lips while looking at my face in the mirror. Who cared what I looked like, anyway?

Someone knocked on my door, and I wondered if Corey was just eager to see me. Before I gave my permission for the entrance, Shauna peeked her head through the door. "Are you coming? The dinner is ready."

"Thank you. I'll be right there."

I felt little butterflies in my stomach. My heart raced. I didn't know how I'd become a prisoner of this house or why I was being captive, but Corey held the answers to my questions. I'd hoped he would tell me good news: the captivity idea was to keep me safe from the outside world, or that he was too possessive of me and didn't want me to leave him. I would consider forgiving him on both accounts, provided he'd give my freedom back. After all, it wasn't like he kept me a prisoner somewhere in a dark and moldy basement. People would kill to live in a house like this.

Downstairs, I found Shauna and Corey chit-chatting about the weather. How that summer was especially hot, with the fire calamities becoming a frequent occurrence in California. They discussed climate change and what the government could do to stop it. When they saw me, they stopped talking, and both looked at me like they'd seen a ghost.

I stopped in the middle of the living room and gave Corey a little wave. "Hi Corey."

"Well, hello, Sam," he said. I didn't know if I should walk up to him to give him a hug. He didn't move, and I remained motionless. "How are you feeling?"

"Good." I nodded my head. "Everything's fine."

"Shauna tells me you're getting comfortable in the house. That's progress."

"Well, yeah." I said. Shauna wasn't saying anything. I felt her eyes glued to me.

"It takes patience, a certain personality to endure what you have. I applaud you for that." I said nothing. "In retrospect and conclusion, I chose the right person."

I shook my head. "I don't understand. Right person for what?"

Corey lifted his index finger and waved it in the air.

"That is an excellent question. I think we all need to be in the right headspace to have that discussion." He turned to Shauna and said, "Don't you think?"

Shauna nodded in agreement and looked like she wanted to say something, but nothing came out of her mouth.

"Well, then. Let's have dinner now and talk later. I'm starving." He grabbed his stomach and tapped it twice.

We all sat down at the table and stared down at our plate. There was enough food for an entire army. Corey occasionally looked up and ordered me to eat. "We need your baby to be strong and healthy. Eat." His voice wasn't sweet. It sounded like a command I had better obey. We ate in silence; an excruciating, painful silence.

I'd gazed in both of their direction every once in a while, and they'd act like everything was normal, like we were one happy family. Anticipation was killing me. I'd stayed quiet for the sake of not ruffling any feathers, or making my situation worse. The thought of finding out the truth was making me dizzy, because what if Corey pronounced I was his prisoner for life? That meant I'd never see my mother or Michelle again? I'd never enjoy the world as gifted by its creator.

Corey ate fast. He'd put a spoonful in his mouth and chew like an animal. I remembered Corey being more civil than this. I refused to show any signs of annoyance.

While I was still picking at my food, Corey turned to Shauna and asked, "What's for dessert?"

"We have cheesecake and chocolate cake. Your favorite." She smiled at him.

"Perfect! Let's all go sit in the living room and relax, shall we?"

I put the plate to the side, stood up from my chair, and walked in the living room direction, hoping my world would soon turn normal again.

CHAPTER FORTY-SIX

We sat in the living room in a circle of chairs, all facing each other. Corey had already devoured his dessert. He looked at me and tilted his head. "Well, Sam, I could only imagine your anxiety to understand what is going on here. You have been quite cooperative, and that is much appreciated." Shauna's advice to listen emerged from my subconscious. I said nothing in return.

Corey stood up and walked to the bar to pour himself a glass of whiskey. He turned to Shauna and offered her one, but she dutifully refused, like a good subordinate. He sat down, holding his whiskey glass with a pinky sticking out. I wondered if he was aware of that little finger wandering in the air. He took a sip and looked at me with squinted eyes—was it the taste of alcohol, or was it something that I'd done to cause that strange look? He crossed his leg over the other and began. When his mouth opened, my stomach felt uneasy, and my mind went numb.

"How old are you, Sam?"

"I recently turned twenty." I said. It annoyed me he

couldn't remember my age. I was sure I told him when we first met.

"Young. So young. When I was your age, I remember. I was already a pilot flying the vast sky and visiting every corner of the globe. I guess I got lucky my career took off so rapidly. But, truth be told, I worked hard for it. I didn't sit around and slack off. I was adamant about fulfilling my goals and doing whatever was needed to advance in life."

Corey sounded preachy for my taste, but it was the opportunity to get to know him better—whether or not I wanted that. He swirled the whiskey around in the glass and a couple of drops escaped the glass rim.

"Let me get to the point. We're going to do an exchange here. A perfect exchange. An exchange you won't be able to resist."

I widened my eyes and wondered what was in store for me.

"Yeah?" I said.

"Yes. It involves your career, Sam. I know how much you've wanted to act. You wanted to be on stage with the famous actors. Be in blockbuster movies. You want to do well in life not to never worry about having a home or affording a new phone. And guess what? You can have all of that. I can give all of it to you if you agree to one thing."

Silence permeated the room, and Shauna beside me was motionless, nearly breathless. Shauna was just a peon, and she did everything Corey asked her to do. Though, come to think of it, asking was a kind word; more like ordering.

"I could get you in touch with Steven Spielberg. I can introduce you to Robert De Niro. Did you say he was your favorite?" He remembered my favorite actor, but not my age. What a dud.

I nodded. "One of my favorites." I still didn't know where Corey was going with all this, but I played along and waited patiently for the verdict.

"In our circles, we call them Stevie and Bobby." He laughed.

I cringed. Bobby was a terrible nickname for my hero actor.

"As for the exchange, I believe you'll agree this is a good deal. For you, for both of us." He cleared his throat and looked at Shauna, who held a stern gaze at Corey the whole time. "Shauna would agree with me that every single person who made a deal was quite happy. Don't you think so, Shauna?"

"Yes. I believe that to be true."

"Will you tell me already what you mean by the exchange?" I fidgeted in my seat, my brows furrowed.

Corey stood up and circled around his chair once—a strange choice of action. He sat down again, his legs uncrossed this time, elbow on his knees, hands supporting his chin. He stared at me for what seemed to be forever and leaned back on his chair, putting on a sly smile. "I think I can trust you, Sam. You're one of those people who'd do anything for their career."

"Perhaps."

"My proposal—and listen to me good—is that while you enjoy your new successful career in acting, I keep the baby. Our baby."

I gasped. "Oh. Oh, my God! Are you serious? This is the exchange?" Corey nodded while keeping his eyes on me. "That... that's fantastic! I was afraid you'd come up with something much worse. Like, you're going to keep me in this house until I die."

Corey laughed. "Oh no. You're not staying in this house a day longer after you give birth. With a modest allowance, I will give you a studio apartment and you're on your own. Of course, your acting career begins as soon as you make an effort. My end of the bargain is to get you connected to the right people. You do the rest."

"Of course. I get it. So, the person you tried to connect me to before—Chris—who is he?"

He waved his hand in dismissal. "He's just my buddy. He knows nothing about the movie industry." I smirked. "But don't worry. A future is in front of you. You'll be a superb actress."

In a flash, the baby photos on the wall came in front of my eyes and I flinched. The baby inside me would end up like the others: plastered to a wall, but in reality—where would he or she go exactly? Corey didn't strike me as a fatherly figure who'd settle to stay home and nourish his child with attention and love. And where were the babies from the wall?

"Thank you. That's quite a compliment." I grabbed the corner of my T-shirt and slightly pulled it against me. "If I may ask, what are you planning to do with this baby?"

"We prefer not to discuss these matters with our clients." Clients? Was I his client now? "Most women who come through end up wanting to keep their child. A motherly instinct or some bullshit like that. But you—you're a perfect example of someone who is neither capable of keeping this child nor simply wanting it." He shrugged. "Shauna informed me you tried an abortion. I'm glad that didn't work out. But it says how much you care about your career more than the baby. Good news for us!"

"That still doesn't tell me what you're doing with the baby."

"Right, right. Curiosity killed the cat, but if you must know... your baby is going to end up with a couple in need. A couple who can't have children. A sad story, indeed."

"A couple? Are you selling the baby?"

Corey laughed so hard that he almost fell off his chair. Then he instantly became serious and looked at me. "Sam, you're too smart for your own good. You better be careful asking too many questions."

"How much money are you getting for this baby?" I involuntarily touched my belly and took off my hand immediately when I realized what I had done. I didn't want Corey or Shauna to think I would protect my unborn child.

"Let's just say enough to retire early. But I won't divulge details to you, my dear. You and I made the exchange, and you ought to be happy."

"Isn't selling people illegal?" I pressed further, risking my stance.

"Illegal? Not if you and I make a deal." Corey crossed his legs and dropped his arms on the sides of the chair's armrests. He looked awfully comfortable for a crime doer. "It's a business like any other. Didn't you hear about those Spanish children back in the 1960s?"

I shook my head. My existence wasn't even planned back then, plus admittedly, our town wasn't best known for learning news or sharing information, old or new.

"Back in the day, while Franco still ruled the country, several hospitals in Spain stole babies and sold them to good families. The nuns who gave birth to these women would tell them their baby was stillborn. The women, of course, were unwed or poor, just like you, so it was quite easy to accomplish this task."

He cleared his throat and continued, "Nobody is sure how many babies were stolen back then, but some estimate tens of thousands. Tens of thousands of babies that found a home. Perhaps Franco was a crazy man, but he made sense. He was a true businessman who got shit done."

"How did it all start?"

"Good question. You always ask good questions, Sam. Sometimes I'm impressed by your intelligence." He crossed his arms. "Franco believed that the babies whose parents were Franco's left-wing opponents had a 'red gene.' His opponents were executed and their wives would end up in prison. Yeah, he was sick, no argument. When the women gave birth to their baby in prison, the babies would be given to the conservative families where they belonged, according to Franco."

As I listened, I felt sick to my stomach, but I kept a poker face. That Corey was some kind of human trafficking lord untangled a lot of the knots. The much bigger shock came the following day, when I encountered a surprise that shook me to my core.

CHAPTER FORTY-SEVEN

I came to peace with my ultimate destiny. I would deliver my child and hand it over to Corey's secret operation. With my hands crossed behind my head, I lay in bed, dreaming about being on the big screen and acting for blockbusters. If Corey was to be trusted, that could be my ticket to a better future.

Downstairs, there was a commotion. A loud uproar of laughter was echoing through the house. Corey had visitors. I stood up from bed and placed my ear next to the door, hoping to hear the conversation. The voices were loud, but not loud enough for me to dissect the words. It seemed like there were two other men besides Corey in the house. As I listened in more carefully, I realised I'd heard those voices before.

"Shit. Could it be?" I whispered to myself, still in disbelief, hoping my memory was wrong.

I had no chance but to come out of my room and make an appearance. Shauna opened the door without knocking and smashed it against me.

"Don't you knock?" I asked.

"What are you doing standing next to the door? I hope you aren't eavesdropping." She had her arms on her waist and she was acting like a scolding mother to a disobedient daughter.

"I wasn't. I was just about to come out of the room and go to the pool."

Without words, she turned around and walked back to the ground floor. I assumed I should have followed her, because her visits in the afternoon usually meant I had to come along wherever she was going.

Downstairs in the living room, Corey was sitting in his chair and chatting with two other men. As I came nearer, the other two men looked familiar. They were all chatting and laughing. When they saw me, the conversation went dead, and they all stared at me.

Unable to speak, I saw Michael first. Next to him sat Brian with repulsion on his face. My heart pounded when I realized Michael had to be part of Corey's crimes. But Brian? I was less surprised about him. The guy always looked creepy, like there was something seriously wrong with him. I couldn't stand him then, and I couldn't stand to look at him now.

"Hey, Sam." Michael was the first one to say some-thing. "It's nice to see you again. You probably thought we'd never cross paths again."

"What are you doing here, Michael?" An unhinged part of me hoped he'd say everything was a big joke and Brian would give me my job back at the Spy Café. How wonderful that would be. Things we take for granted seemed like splendid gifts in dire circumstances. I gazed at

Brian and he seemed uninterested in either seeing me or adding to the conversation.

"This is our meeting place. Our headquarter." He looked around the room and smiled. "I hope you've enjoyed the house. We put some effort into making it comfortable, but I understand it's painful without the amenities such as cable or Wi-Fi. People—or should I say, women—get used to it, eventually. They become quite introspective when they spend lots of time alone."

"Wait," I gazed at Corey, "You don't live here?"

Corey shook his head and smiled. At least that explained the empty closets in the main bedroom.

"As a matter of fact," Michael continued, "none of us do."

My legs were shaking beneath me and I needed to sit down. Corey noticed me getting uncomfortable and offered me a seat. I leaned against the chair, hiding an involuntary sigh.

"Michael could have lived here, like me, should you have gone out on a date with him." Corey gestured quotation marks with his hands up in the air with the word "lived."

"What do you mean?" I said.

"He asked you on a date multiple times and you refused it. They had to bring me to lure you in. I guess you go for muscular guys." He turned to Michael. "No offense, buddy."

Michael waved his hand to dismiss his joke. "No offense taken," he confirmed. Michael looked thinner and more handsome than I remembered him. Or my memory tricked me again. He exuded more confidence, as if he was on his true turf and had nothing to worry about.

"But Michael has found other girls to date who will be cooperative. Right, Michael?"

He laughed. "It never fails."

"Mind if I sit?" I said.

"Not at all," Corey and Michael said in unison.

I was facing the three criminals, and I was shaking in fear. Shauna had left the room and was nowhere to be found. The three men stared at me, expecting me to say something, but I lost the right words.

"This is all so well-orchestrated." I said. "I wish you'd talked to me about this instead of sneaking the plan on me."

Corey and Michael looked at each other, and Michael gave a nod to Corey, as if giving him permission to answer.

"A woman like you would never agree to this deal unless she was already pregnant. It's a human nature. But you have no choice now that the baby exists." All three men fell into an uproarious laugh. Shauna reappeared and asked what was so funny, but they kept laughing, unable to speak.

I grabbed the chair armrests with all my might and said, "I'm sorry, gentlemen, but I need to lie in bed and rest. Pregnancy does this." I stood up and smiled at Michael and Corey and proceeded to my room. I felt all the eyes staring at my back in silence. Then Michael spoke. "Next time I see you, consider giving a hug."

CHAPTER FORTY-EIGHT

Discovering Michael's true persona made me sick to my stomach, and the betrayal stung, despite only having known him for a week. Nothing about him had given off criminal vibes, and I cringed at the thought of their manipulation. The expanse of time I had in which to do nothing but think made it hard to avoid going over it and over it in my head.

Michael had attempted to court me and take me out on dates with the same intention that Corey had. But when I kept refusing him, they'd brought in Corey to charm me into his world. Corey kept giving me empty promises to connect me with those who can help me with my acting. Corey sent me flowers and took me out to dinners—it was all a perfect plan. And then, the icing on the cake, Brian fired me, so I would panic and seek help from the closest person I had. I was naïve, and my false optimism had got me into trouble.

The following days, Shauna kept a close eye on me, closer than before. Whenever I went outside to the backyard, she'd be right behind me, asking me if I needed something. If I walked around the house out of boredom, she'd follow me with her eyes and inquire about my plans for the day.

But truth be told, I had no plans. I wandered around like a lost soul, waiting for the last act of this play. At least, they'd guaranteed my release from this place. Freedom— the one true thing guaranteed in life could not be taken for granted. Shauna did what she had to do. In a way, they'd compromised her freedom, too. She was locked in this scheme, voluntarily or not, and she would watch ladies grow their bellies for as long as the business prospered.

One day, Shauna allowed me to wander into the back- yard farther from the house. She seemed busy that morn- ing, moving the furniture around, doing the laundry, and cooking multiple meals. Whenever she needed a mood boost, she played music in the house, and I caught her once dancing to an imaginary mic in her hand. Shauna knew I couldn't get away or go far. The only space I could occupy was the premises, and it was fenced all around. The weather was beckoning, and I wished I could spend time outside of the house. I longed for Michelle's company and her cute laughter. Even Mother would be a welcome addi- tion to my daily life. I was tired of the same views, same company, same air.

I walked until I noticed a small hill near the hedges. Out of curiosity, I came up and kneeled down to check it out. The top of the pile had no grass, but the rains had packed the dirt. I started digging with my hands until I removed most of the dirt. Under my fingertips, I felt something hard, and I kept digging. I unearthed a bone, and I let out a yelp in surprise. I sat on the grass to compose my thoughts. The bone was protruding from the ground, bare and white. I continued to dig and found more and more. Enough to make up a full skeleton.

A human skeleton.

Shocked, I covered my mouth with my hand to stop myself from screaming. In the back of my mind, I heard my biology teacher in high school, Mr. Williams, tell us all about skeletonization.

In warmer climates, skeletonization could happen in a few weeks, whereas in the colder weather an entire year. Everything around me started to spin and bile rose inside me, burning the back of my throat.

These human remains must have been here longer than a few weeks. Who were they, and how did they end up here? I could, literally, be in grave danger. Corey's deal sounded empty next to the unofficial grave of human remains. I had to escape.

I felt someone watching me from behind, and I turned around, looking at the house. A curtain on one window moved, and I was certain it was Shauna watching me.

I shoveled the dirt with my hands back to the pile, and I ran back to the house. I rushed through the house to my room, hoping Shauna wouldn't see my dirty hands. Luckily, she didn't appear, even though I felt her eyes on me from around a corner.

As soon as I entered my room, I shuffled to the bathroom and scrubbed my dirty hands. I dug into my cuticles to ensure no dirt remained. Tears flooded down my cheeks as I pictured the ill-faith of the person—or people—lying below the ground. Spent and exhausted, I went to my bed and curled up, my mind circling again and again around the horror I'd found.

Later that day, Michael arrived at the house alone. Shauna must have told him what I'd discovered. I heard Shauna and Michael having a rowdy conversation downstairs. Corey was gone for a couple of days, and he was no longer informing me of his whereabouts. My room walls were comfortable and familiar, like an old commercial jingle we hear as adults. Whenever guests came, I was reluctant to face them.

Michael stormed into my room without knocking and when he saw me, he said, "I'm glad you're here."

"Where else would I be?" I said.

"I don't know. Wandering around and being nosy."

I scoffed. "I have no interest in either."

I focused my gaze on the pattern of the curtains.

"What's the matter?"

"Nothing." I didn't feel like seeing or speaking to Michael. He came close to my bed and hovered over me.

"Hey, if it isn't clear, I want to mention that all this operation, our exchange deal, is top secret. Once we complete the exchange, you're free to go, and go on with your life. We will never see each other again. If you leak any information about this to anyone, you're dead. Understood? Dead. We will find you wherever you are. You won't be able to hide from me."

I looked up at him and saw his face contorted into rage.

"Don't worry. I won't."

"Good." He said and stormed out of the room.

CHAPTER FORTY-NINE

As time moved on, the only thing that changed was my growing belly. October came, and the heat seemed to have eased a bit. As a pregnant person, the heat didn't suit me well. I'd kept having to stop to catch my breath in the scorching temperatures.

Leslie came by every so often and checked my blood pressure, took my blood, and monitored the growth of the baby, listening to the heartbeat. The results were always good, and it was no surprise coming from a young and healthy woman like me. I'd probed Shauna to take me to the proper hospital, to be checked up on by actual doctors, but she claimed the trip could be risky, given my captivity. They didn't trust me.

One day, Leslie came by to make an important announcement. I was sitting in the backyard, staring at the hedges in front of me and feeling the time go by, when she stormed into the house and screamed, "It's a boy, it's a boy."

I turned around to see Leslie walk into the kitchen to grab a bottle of champagne to toast with Shauna. Uninterested, I turned back around and kept staring at the hedges. Was the price of a boy higher than that of a girl? The gender didn't matter to me. The child was destined for another family, and I didn't need to worry whether to buy blue or pink clothes, or what color to paint the nursery walls.

Leslie and Shauna were clinking their glasses and giggling. They paid me no attention. Beyond the hedges, there was a voice, subtle and serene, calling me. "Sam. Sam, come."

I propped myself up in the chair as if looking beyond the hedges, but there was nobody on the other side. The voice continued to linger in the air. Then a laugh, which was beautiful and Song-like. "Sam." Then I heard a laugh. "Sam, darling. Come, I want to tell you something."

I stood up from my chair and took small steps forward. My curiosity grew as the voice beckoned me to come. But the voice turned serious. "Sam, hurry! You're moving slow."

I quickened my steps until my feet ran. When I approached the hedges, the voice whispered and I couldn't make out what it was saying. Like a savage, with both hands, I reached for the hedges and moved them around, trying to see the end; to find the person desperately trying to get to the other side.

"Sam!" A voice behind me was so close it startled me. "Sam, what on earth are you doing?" Shauna grabbed my left arm and pulled me towards the house. I smelled the champagne in her mouth; the drink celebrating my son. Wide-eyed, I looked at her, unable to give her an explanation. My silence seemed to have irked her even more, and she pulled me with all her might.

I fell to the ground and seconds later, Leslie was running towards us, screaming, "Oh my God, is she okay?"

"She's okay." Shauna sounded angry. "Your attempt to escape is unacceptable. We have made a deal and you will not try to break it."

Surprised to hear my voice, I said, "Sorry. I thought I had heard someone calling me. I think I heard my mother, but I'm not sure."

Shauna smirked and said, "You're just imagining things. Your pregnancy must be making you out of sorts."

Both women took me by the armpit on each side and dragged me up. I gazed at Leslie and thought I saw a tear in her eye. As we walked through the lawn towards the house, Shauna said I'd be under close supervision from now on. What that meant, as I later found, was that she would keep me in my room locked and bring me food and water three times a day.

She escorted me to my room, left, and locked the door behind her.

CHAPTER FIFTY

I was entirely lost in time. Only the cooler weather gave me clues it could be a fall. Days were getting shorter and the sound of crickets outside became less frequent. I counted on my fingers the number of months left to deliver—I thought there were three, four left—but I wasn't entirely sure my math stood correct. I only knew that the baby sent kicks once in a while, moving around my body as if seeking the most comfortable spot.

My tiredness was mostly gone, and I had enough energy to exist but no activities to stimulate me because of being closed in my room all the time. Every once in a while, Shauna would let me eat in the kitchen, but she'd sit across from me and watch me closely. Those moments grew awkward, not just because we did everything in silence from the day she'd locked me up in the room, but because we both knew this was going to end and it was temporary and senseless.

"We're having a party tonight."

"What's the party for?" I took the nibble at a chance of a conversation, desperate to connect to another human.

"Today is Halloween. We have a Halloween party here every year. It's become a tradition."

"Oh. How many people are coming?"

Shauna paused to think, as if she was counting in her head, and said, "About twenty-five."

I nodded. "That's decent."

"I expect you to be in your room the entire time."

I didn't think the party would make any difference. Shauna would keep me locked in my room, anyway.

Shauna's forehead was even more furrowed than usual, and she had a faraway look in her eyes. She seemed distracted. Perhaps even distressed. I hadn't seen her in this state before. Shauna was always in command of her feelings and emotions. Her foot was tapping against the floor and she gazed at my plate as I moved the food around. She looked at her watch and said, "Why are you playing with your food? Are you done with it?"

"Yes," I confirmed.

"Okay, let's go upstairs. I don't have a minute to spare."

As we walked up the stairs to my little prison, I turned around and asked Shauna over my shoulder, "What's your costume going to be?"

She didn't answer right away, but she squeezed an answer through her thoughts. "A nurse."

"Oh, how fun." She didn't respond, but ordered me to be quiet in the room when the guests arrived. "But I'm always quiet."

"Sure, unless you talk to voices in your head."

With that, she closed the door and walked away. Did she not lock the door this time? After she'd moved enough to know there was a safe distance between us, I reached for the doorknob and the door opened up. Yes!

A couple of hours later, when I heard guests downstairs, I stole out of my room and plodded down the hallway. I came close to the railing and kneeled down for cover. I saw the people down below in their Halloween costumes, carefree, laughing, cracking jokes, and touching each other. Batman and Mario were having what seemed to be a serious conversation in a corner of the room. Baby Shark was lurking around and walking in circles as if a real shark. Then there was Shauna—a nurse. The costume was supposed to be sexy, but it didn't suit her well. The front door opened and my heart skipped a beat when Corey showed up in his cop costume. Not just because I was always afraid of cops, even just a sight of them, but because under his arm was a woman dressed as a ballerina. She had long dark hair and looked like she'd stepped out of a magazine. I squinted my eyes to see her face a little better from this distance, and I saw a radiant face; a smile that disarmed. He kissed her on the lips and released her arm slowly, as if it was difficult to separate, then walked to the kitchen. Jealousy rushed over me even though I should be the last person to feel jealous of Corey's lady. She went on her merry way and hugged every single person in the room. They all seemed like a tight group of friends, like a clan with a purpose.

I stood up quickly, feeling dizzy from the move, and went back to my room. I stripped the white sheet from the bed and frantically looked for a sharp object to make two holes. In the bathroom, I found an old razer and slowly chipped at the material of the sheet to make two small holes. It took forever, but it was worth the risk.

Hours must have passed since I discovered my room was unlocked. Shauna never came to see me, although her usual time was around ten to ask me if I was hungry. The uproar downstairs went up by a few decibels. The music was loud enough to hear they were playing a mix of hip-hop and soul. There was laughter and chatter, and the clicking of glasses. No one came upstairs to check up on me or say hello.

The sheet was too much big for my stature, so after I'd placed it over my head, I took a belt from my luggage and placed it around my waist to hold the sheet in place. With slight apprehension, my hands visibly shaking, I moved forward with opening the door and walking toward the mass of costumes. My peripheral vision was not there as I could only look through the small holes in the sheet, but I could see enough to distinguish a cop and a nurse.

At the bottom of the stairs, I appeared ghostly in my new attire. No one seemed to have noticed the unfamiliar presence of a costume that seemed odd and out of place. Everyone just paid attention to their own activity, oblivious to their surroundings. I looked at the clock in the hallway and saw it was eleven at night. It was no surprise that the party would be a drunken, careless, and jolly affair.

I moved across the section of the room when there were the fewest people on the floor and headed for the door. Outside, a fresh scent of autumn splashed over me. Several fancy cars were parked in the cul-de-sac. The trees nearby lost their leaves and turned into giant combs. I turned around to see if anyone had noticed or watched me, but the path was clear and no one was there. At the gate, I noticed two colossal statues as Halloween decorations. I couldn't tell what they were from a distance, but when I

THE EXCHANGE: A NOVEL

came close to one, a large old witch was looking out the gate. I took the sheet off of me and packed it deep into the hedges next to the gate. I stood next to the witch, my whole body shaking from fear. Any second now, Shauna could catch me and send me back to my prison.

Like a miracle dropping from the sky, only a few minutes later, a set of car headlights was beaming onto the gate. The gravel beneath the tires was crackling like a fire and getting closer. The gates mechanics made a noise and the gate slowly opened. The car proceeded through the gate, and while they were still open, I plunged toward the small gap and found myself on the other side—free. The car took off at high speed and nothing but the dark path and shrubs and trees surrounded me.

For the strangest reason, Stacey's words came to mind: perish or persist. I had no time to think: it was time to persist.

In shock and disbelief about my newfound freedom, my feet shuffled themselves to a safe place. I didn't bother to look around; I ran and ran and ran until I came across the intersection with a car stopped at the red light. I approached it and banged on the passenger window. "Please help me, please."

A woman in her thirties opened the door and yelled for me to get in. Just as I positioned myself in the seat, the light turned green and the woman drove in silence, occasionally looking at me, listening to my attempt to catch my breath.

When I came to my senses a mile later, she asked, "Are you okay?" She sounded concerned and curious and annoyed all at once. I didn't know if I was okay. I was far from the dreadful house, and that was all mattered.

"Yes. Thank you. I need a phone, please. Can I borrow yours?"

She took her phone out of her back pocket, unlocked it with the password, and handed it to me. "Here you go."

I dialed the numbers slowly—only then did I notice my hands visibly shaking. The line on the other side rang. "Hello?" My mother sounded utterly depressed and lifeless.

In shock at hearing my mother's voice, I could not speak at first. Her dull voice made it through again, "Hello, who is this?" Maybe she had been waiting for me all along. Maybe she was looking for news from whomever or wherever.

"Mom, it's me."

"Sam." She burst into tears.

"Mom, come get me. Take me home."

CHAPTER FIFTY-ONE

Mother found me at the Union Station like I had asked her to. I sat curled up near the curbside, feeling homeless. Her Jeep pulled in and her hand waved at me to come in. Wearily, I opened the door and almost sobbed at the sight of my mother sitting at the wheel, smiling at me. "Darling, I'm so happy you called."

Mother wavered as she drove. She had no clue where she was going. Tears covered her face, and she kept her speed slow, taking care not to get us into a car accident. She stayed way below the speed limit, and looked at me once in a while, letting her tears fall all over again.

She gazed ahead above the steering wheel rim, as if in deep thought.

The second she'd hung up from our phone call the morning of my escape, she'd ran to her car and drove. Except to refill the tank with gas, she'd made no stops on her twelve-hour ride. She looked exhausted after the sleepless night. With eyes half-closed, she finally broke the silence.

"Sweetie, are you... are you pregnant?" I could no longer hide the fact there was a baby inside my body. I nodded, but my mother didn't catch my gesture. "Are you?" she said again.

"I am."

"Oh, dear. I'm going to be a grandmother." She released one hand from the wheel and put it on her mouth as she sobbed.

"Mom, why don't we stop in a motel somewhere and rest up? You look like you could use some rest."

Her eyes twinkled with hope. "Okay. That sounds good. Let's find a motel and stay."

We got on I-40 East and drove until we hit Ontario. My mother took the first exit and asked me to look for a suitable motel for us to stay in. A few miles down the main street, the dim lights of the Motel 6 sign drew my attention. Mother pulled over in the parking lot next to the motel, got out of the car, and stood next to it, staring at the motel as if she'd seen a ghost. I came around and grabbed her hand. "Mom, let's go. Let's get you some rest."

"Yeah." She shuffled behind me, looking down at the ground.

We settled in a room on the first floor, overlooking the busy main street. Ontario was a small town with a single motel, a gas station, and a grocery store all in their proximity. My mother fell into her bed, with her eyes glued to the ceiling. I watched her unfold her exhaustion as her eyes closed.

I lay sideways in the bed next to hers, my elbow folded, my face leaning on my hand.

"Hey, Mom."

Her heavy eyes opened up and gazed at me. "Yes?"

"What did you think when you didn't hear from me for months?"

She bubbled up a bit by putting on a small smile and widening her eyes. "I felt bad. I felt terrible, Sam."

"You did. Why?"

"We had that argument, and I thought you were mad at me this whole time."

"Mom, really? You thought I was mad at you for five months?"

"I'm sorry, Sam. I'm a terrible mother."

"I'm not saying you're a terrible mother. Mom, I am trying to understand what happened here. Did you try to contact me at all?"

"I did." She responded fast, as if in self-defense. "Of course, I did. But every time I called, it would go right into your voicemail. I thought you were sending my calls there."

"Mom, did you consider calling the police? See if I could be somewhere dead?"

"Oh. Don't say that." She paused as her eyes shot all over the ceiling. "I have faith. God kept you safe. I trusted him."

I rolled my eyes. "God could save me to the extent I could save myself, Mom. Sure, God doesn't kill people. But people kill people. Do you think God could save me from other people?"

"I have faith. I have faith." She looked at me as tears rolled down her cheeks.

" So, you didn't call the police?"

She shook her head. "No, no, darling. I didn't call the police. You would call me eventually, I knew that. I was waiting for your call. I felt you were still alive."

Mother wasn't interested in what happened. She didn't ask me who the father of my child was. She didn't ask me why she couldn't reach me on the phone. She didn't even bother to know how I was feeling at that moment. Maybe that I was still alive was overwhelming enough for her. I never found out why. And she never found out a word about my captivity.

Silence fell between us until Mother let out a snore. She'd fallen asleep.

"Mom!" My shout startled her. She propped herself up with her eyes wide open.

"What?"

"Listen to me, Mom. As soon as we get home, I want you to take me to the hospital."

"Okay, Sam. I can do that. I will do whatever you ask me to do."

"Mom, I don't want the baby." I knew it was late for an abortion, but I wanted to make plans to put the baby up for an adoption.

"Sam. Oh, Sam." Mother got off the bed and, with tears in her eyes, came to me and kneeled next to me. Her hands landed on my stomach. "Please, please, Sam. Don't get rid of this child. Give me another chance. I will be a wonderful grandmother. Please, Sam." Her voice crackled through her tears.

I watched the back of Mother's head as she kissed my belly. I put my hand on her hair and gently padded it.

CHAPTER FIFTY-TWO

We woke up early in the morning and ate breakfast and drank coffee in our room. Our trip home was going to be at least ten hours long. Mother seemed hesitant to speak, gazing at me tentatively, hoping I wouldn't catch her eyes. She was clearly skirting around some kind of news she wanted to deliver, as she kept opening her mouth and closing it again. She had a sadness about her. Her droopy eyes gave away heaviness. I knew her well enough that she had something to say, but she didn't know how. She dropped her eyes to the ground again and shake her head.

"What is it, Mother? Is there something you want to tell me?" I swallowed the ball of nerves that was lodged in my throat.

She held her hands up near her torso. "It's Michelle."

Judging by Mother's tone, it was bad news, but I didn't know how bad it was. I was feeling sick to my stomach. "What about Michelle?"

"She..." Mother's eyes looked around, as if trying to

find a comfortable spot. They avoided mine. "She took her own life."

My body dropped onto the bed as if someone pushed me. Out of nowhere, an uncontrollable laughter came from inside me. The laugh was hysterical. I turned to the side to see my mother staring at me with her mouth wide open. The laughter carried on until it turned to sobs. I closed my eyes with my hands and felt the wetness from my tears. Mother sat next to me and caressed my hair. She, too, cried.

My best friend Michelle was gone. She was like a sister. She was my best friend. The last time I saw her was the day before I left for L.A. The last image I had of her—her sad and nostalgic eyes—kept returning, and I hated myself for not asking her how she was doing, or whether there was anything I could do for her. Was she happy? If I could have at least offered to share her pain.

Mother held a piece of paper in her hand and handed it over.

Through my tears, I asked, "What is this?"

"Michelle's mother found a note Michelle left. It's for you."

I didn't think I was ready for this, but I grabbed the paper out of my mother's hand and opened it. I immediately recognized Michelle's messy cursive writing. I'd seen it so many times when we passed notes in the classroom and giggled at scribblings.

The note said:

Dear Sam, I hope you're reading this happy and satisfied in L.A. I hope you're living the dream you've had since you were a child. Acting was your favorite, and you will succeed someday, I know this. I've tried to contact you several times over the phone

and social media since you left, but lately, all my calls have gone
unanswered. I just assumed you were busy with life. That's what
happens to those who are climbing up in the world.

As for me? I've decided it is time for me to go. I feel an inde-
scribable weight on my chest. It feels heavy, and I don't know how
to get rid of it. Also, this town is not conducive to happiness and
joy. You understand that the best. I admire your courage to leave
and get out there to be somebody. I've found no courage to move on.
My life is empty, and no prospects show on the horizon. The world
of eight billion people as of now does not need a lonely sad me. I
know that all my pain and sadness will disappear once the black
curtain comes down. I look forward to that.

Try to live the best and most decent life for both of us. I will
see you on the other side, my friend. With love, Michelle

As I read the note, I wiped my tears and sniffled.
Mother sat next to me, hoping I'd read it out loud. I
brought the note next to my chest and looked up at the
ceiling, hoping Michelle was happy in heaven. Later, my
mother told me they'd found her in her bedroom; she had
hung herself.

The news of a young woman taking her own life reverberated with shock around our small town. The old church
ladies claimed the devil possessed Michelle and stole her
soul. Her parents were filled with sadness and grief, some
shame mixed in. They couldn't explain what went wrong
with an only child of theirs. They couldn't fathom the
depths of despair she must have fallen to. In a short few
months, they separated after realizing their daughter was
the staple of their small nuclear family. She was the glue
that had dried off and caused the pieces to break and fall. I
only knew I would terribly miss her. My dear Michelle. I
longed to hug her one last time.

Mother consoled me and kept saying I had to keep strong for my baby. She said she couldn't wait to get me home and care for me and her grandson. Now that I associated the motel room with the death of my only friend, I couldn't wait to head through the door. We had no luggage to carry or worry about. We had nothing to hold in our hands except the heaviness of life upon us.

CHAPTER FIFTY-THREE

NOW

I drive Jake to the community pool a few blocks away from our house. It's the only place I can come up with. Gallup doesn't have many community pools or lakes or ponds for heat reprieves. I look around several times before I jump in my car and search for evidence of the car with tinted windows. I'm feeling nervous, and can't wait to arrive at the pool. The day is scorching and unbearable. The grass looks yellow and unredeemable. A perfect day for a swim and splash. When we arrive, the pool is packed, and it looks like everyone is elbowing each other inside. I am lucky, because chairs are still available for rental. At the ticket stand at the entrance, I look up and see a camera. Being watched has been my least favorite since L.A. I lower my head down and adjust my sunglasses on my nose.

Jake runs to the pool and jumps in. I pay for my chair.

I go lie down on my rented chair and place a straw hat on my face. The sun's rays burn my skin but I enjoy it even though I suspect I will pay for it in blisters later. The children scream in their playfulness and they lull me to slumber. Minutes pass, but I don't have a clue how many. Children keep screaming and, as I open my eyes, I cringe at their high-pitch voices.

I give another look around the pool to scan the faces of the adults. In my subconscious, I expect to see Corey or one of his posse watching us over. I only see the parents I don't recognize, and they don't recognize me. That is what I prefer. Since I returned home, I've been incognito, minding my own business.

Most of the time, I am scared someone is watching me. I fear they came to claim what they think is theirs. Jake's voice, if he is screaming, is subdued by the others. Jake. Where is he? I should check in on him. It is this habit of mine I developed to do that often.

I remove my hat and sit up. I scan around the pool for Jake, but he is nowhere to be found. A few adults are standing at the edge of the pool and watching their younglings have fun. I look for Jake. At one point, all the children resemble each other with wet hair glued to their skull, and spotting him is impossible. I stand up and walk to the pool to get a better vantage point. I join the other parents and move closer to the edge of the pool, looking for Jake, but I don't see him.

This is not like Jake—even though he is only four, he is way mature beyond his age and he'd do nothing stupid. I feel lucky that he always obeys me and never questions me. He is quite an easy and amendable child.

After I inspect the entire pool, I panic. Where could

Jake be? I have seen no evidence of an adult pulling a child out of the pool and walking away.

"Jake!" My voice travels along the pool, somewhat muffled by the children's yelps. "Jake!" I scream a little harder and feel eyes staring at me.

"Jake! Jake, where are you?" I try again, because I am now desperate to be heard.

The lifeguard jumps from the watching platform and runs up to me. "Ma'am, you're looking for someone?"

"Yes. I'm looking for my son, Jake. I can't find him." I extend my arms toward the pool as if I am about to dive in. "Please. Please find him."

The lifeguard walks up to a megaphone and places it on his lips, "Jake! Jake, come out of the pool right now!" The children pause for a second and stare in the lifeguard's direction, but none even flinch. Then the commotion continues as if nothing is going on. "Will Jake come out of the pool now? Jake, please come out of the pool." The voice is loud and clear. But no Jake shows up.

I form an anguished look on my face. The man asks me what Jake looks like, and I give him a vague description. A lot of blonde boys with blue eyes are in the pool. He nods and looks at all the boys with blue eyes and blonde hair.

He points an index finger at a boy resembling Jake and asks me, "Is this him?"

I shake my head and let a tear out. With both hands on my mouth, I am shocked and alarmed, and I don't understand where Jake can be. I yell out his name twice for good measure, but my voice sounds shaky.

"Everybody, come out of the pool. Right now!" The lifeguard's voice through the megaphone dominates the block. I don't mean to cause all this commotion, but the situation is dire. "Come out of the pool right now!"

The children, lined up, inch toward the exit, some having trouble to move fast and keep their balance. I stand there and watch them push each other, give each other mean looks, angry about the interruption of their play.

Several minutes pass until the pool is empty. Some people gather their kids and leave while others stand by the pool wondering what is happening and what will transpire in the next few minutes. The pool is now empty, and I still see no evidence of my Jake.

A large man in swimming trunks comes out of the building next to the pool and calls for the lifeguard to jump in. "Scott, look for him inside."

Scott jumps into the pool and swims at the bottom. Both men search for Jake, one inside the pool and the other above, but he doesn't turn up.

The lifeguard resurfaces from the bottom of the pool a few minutes later and announces, "I see nothing. I searched the entire pool."

I cannot move, as the reality is setting in. Jake is lost. Or kidnapped. Or he ran away? No, no. He couldn't have run away. He is a good boy and he would never do such a thing. Good and obedient. A mama's boy. A little angel. How can I lose him like this? I haven't been the best mother, I admit, but the missing of Jake overwhelms me.

The large man approaches me and tells me, "Ma'am, we did our due diligence to find your son, but we couldn't find him. Are you sure he was in the pool last?"

"Yes, yes, he was in the pool last." I say. Tears are filling up my eyes. I cannot stop them.

"Is it possible he came out of the pool and left?"

"It's possible, but that's not Jake-like. He would come right to me if he was tired of swimming." I look around, expecting to see Jake any second.

"I'm very sorry, but there's nothing more we can do. If you're certain that he's missing, call the police." He places his hand on my shoulder. I feel its weight. "Do you want us to call the cops for you?"

The pool looks empty and as smooth as glass. One can now see the floor of the pool, covered in blue tiles. It is as crystal clear as the fact that Jake is nowhere to be found.

I stand motionless and let the sun blind my eyes from the reflection of the pool.

"No, no. I'll call." In my mind, I choose to drive to the police station instead. I don't trust phones.

My head is spinning. I clench my fists. Jake's voice is echoing in my ears, "Mommy, I'm here. Come get me."

But when the large man taps me on the shoulder to tell me the pool is closing for the day and I need to leave, I realize Jake's voice is just a delusion.

Only one thought crosses my mind. Corey. It must be Corey who kidnapped Jake.

CHAPTER FIFTY-FOUR

I close my eyes briefly and thank God the police station isn't too far from the community pool. I drive more slowly than usual in fear I'd hit something from feeling shaky. When I arrive at the police station, I sit in my car and stare at the entrance, wondering if Steve is here today. Steve, my high-school friend, graduated from the police academy three years ago and has become a beloved cop in our town.

I step out of the car on the hot pavement, and the heat hits me immediately. My heart is racing, and all I can see in my mind's eye is Jake. I'm not sure how I'm going to get the words out to Steve. He likes Jake—he stops by our house during his patrolling in the neighborhood and brings him a lollipop or a small toy. The two of them bonded, making me wonder what it would have been like if Jake had a father who'd care for him and love him like I did.

Just as I cross the door, the sobs burst out of me. The woman at the front desk gets up from her chair and asks me if I'm okay. Or, at least, I think that's what she said.

Through my tears, I tell her I need to see Steve. The woman is old, and it looks like she's been with the police station for a long time. Her reassuring tone and firm touch make me believe she's completely in command of the situation. I look at her profile as we walk side by side. She looks stoic and stares ahead, not blinking at all. The woman grabs my arm and squeezes it hard. I say nothing because I have no more words left. She ushers me to Steve's office, which I've never been in before. I've had no reason to visit him at the police station in this small town of next to no crime.

Steve is talking on the phone and when he sees me, he finishes the call and runs toward me. "Sam, are you okay?"

The woman lets my arm go. "You know each other?"

"Yes," Steve says. "We're high school friends." I sense pride in his voice, but I can't return his smile. I can't ever imagine smiling again; not until I have Jake back in my arms. The woman walks out of the office, and Steve closes the door behind her.

"What's going on, buddy?" He always calls me buddy as a way to confirm that's what we are and always will be.

I cup my face with my hands and continue crying. In the corner of my eye, I see Steve, his hand on my arm, waiting for me to say something.

"Jake..."

"What about Jake?" His voice changes to an investigative one.

"They have kidnapped Jake."

He caresses my hand while staying calm.

"Sam, I need you to calm down and tell me everything. When was the last time you saw Jake?"

I wipe my tears from my face, and I take a deep breath

to calm myself. My legs are shaking so much they can barely support my weight, and they're about to give up. "Can I sit down?"

"Of course." He pulls the chair on the other side of his desk and sits down across from me. He leans forward. "Tell me everything."

"Jake and I went to the community pool." I shake my head, still in shock. Sweat is pouring down my back and I keep having to force myself to gulp down air. "I... I closed my eyes. I don't know how long for. I was watching him, and then before I knew it... It couldn't have been more than five minutes. Then a strange feeling came over me, as if someone was looking at me." I check Steve's face expression, but it remains the same. "I snapped out of my nap and I started looking for Jake in the pool, but he was nowhere to be found."

A huge lump forms in my throat. I fight tears back.

"What happened then?"

"The bodyguards emptied the pool, finding no traces of Jake." I cry again.

Steve swings in his chair and turns to the window. I try to slow my racing heart as I wait for Steve's next step.

He picks up his walkie-talkie and orders a search through the town. "Notify the state police and be on the lookout." The device crackles between him and the voice on the other side. They have a full conversation while Steve gives all the pertinent information about my son and his last whereabouts. Eye color, hair color, age. He turns around to face me, his mouth set in a serious line, same as it always is when something important is at stake.

He looks at me and says, "All hands are on deck. Sam, I want to assure you I will do everything in my power to find Jake. Anything I can do for you, you know where to find me."

I nod while looking down at the floor. I look up, and I watch his face, a recent buzz cut that makes his eyes seem bigger. While we stare at each other, I say, "Steve, I think it's Corey. A man named Corey kidnapped Jake."

CHAPTER FIFTY-FIVE

No one could have foreseen Jake's kidnapping except for me. I haven't told a soul what happened in L.A. Now that I've lost my only confidant in life, my dear friend Michelle, I have had no one to talk to. Jake has changed my mother profoundly, but we're still not close enough for me to tell her all my secrets. I was still keeping my darkest secret; the one about Father and what I did on that terrible day after staring at that patch on his head. An unusual activity took place the week leading to Jake's disappearance, and I have no one to talk to about it. A car with California license plates patrolled around my neighborhood, like a bird flying above zeroing out on a tree to nest. The glass windows were tinted black without a hint of who it could be inside. The car had moved slowly, like a lion making its advance to the prey. I saw it parked near the house once, bringing me to full panic mode. Jake was spending time at my mother's place. She had him over at least twice a week, practicing her love and kindness to redeem herself.

I had no evidence the car belonged to Corey's crew.

Only my instinct told me so. Until then, I have seen cars stalking people only in movies. It surprised me it took them four long years to find us. I'd always thought the criminal mind was more sophisticated in plotting evil schemes and executing them swiftly. But the world was enormous, and maybe four years was reasonable after all. Their presence made me fear every move I made. Whenever I was out and about, a strange feeling of eyes being peeled on me followed me. Each day, I'd pick up Jake from daycare at the most unusual hours to trick them into my routine. I'd take him to my mother's place, thinking he was safer in her apartment.

But the day Jake disappeared, the car with the tinted windows would no longer show up in the neighborhood. The news about Jake going missing spread far and wide. The flyers with his innocent little face hung on many trees and light poles around the town.

———

Jake grew into a beautiful boy. At his tender age of almost four, he's always witty and clever in his remarks. He's my constant source of laughter, a lightness that only the innocent can project. He laughs a lot and never complains, although we live a modest life. His existence derailed my career plans. There's no doubt about that, but being a mother brought out an indescribable desire to give him love. Whether it was due to an instinct or my triumphant survival of the captivity, keeping him was the right thing to do.

Jake and I have visited places that satisfy his endless curiosity, such as children's museums, parks, restaurants...

Wherever we go, people smile at and greet him, and children flock to him like he's a magnet.

He and I live in the house I grew up in. Mother still lives in Gallup in her modest apartment. All the house furniture my grandparents bought is still in the house. It looks its age, and reminds me of my grandparents and my father, but neither my mother nor I could afford to replace it. When my mother brought me home from L.A., she had me settle in the house. It wasn't my first choice, but after everything I had experienced, the feeling of familiarity warmed my heart.

Mother doesn't understand why Jake has been kidnapped. I haven't told her anything. She only knows what everyone else does—Jake is nowhere to be found. She wants to visit the house every day, but I tell her it's unnecessary. In fact, I don't want her here every day. She calls me on the phone and speculates about his disappearance. It only makes me angry. I listen, but her worrying doesn't help me, nor will it bring Jake back.

Steve calls every day to keep me posted. He says everything seems strange. Strange, because there are no leads to his disappearance. He says the FBI is now involved, and they will come to my house to question me. He advises me to be as transparent as possible. I tell him it's in my interest to tell the truth. I will do anything to help catch that son of a gun.

CHAPTER FIFTY-SIX

A few months after I gave birth to Jake, I needed to find a job. I looked like a train wreck and borderline unemployable, but I got a job at a children's bookstore in Gallup. The store owner gave me a pass only because I was a mother and a local. The kids would come to the store, and I would entertain them by imitating Goofy and Mickey Mouse. My acting career has been reduced to that. The little cute faces laughed at my silly disposition, and their giggles made me happy.

Almost a week has gone by, and Jake is still missing. My boss has given me some leave, as I'm not in a fit state to work. I'm not sure if I ever will be. My patience is growing thin, but I practice calmness.

It is Saturday, beautiful and inviting outside. I'm having my coffee in the kitchen when someone rings the doorbell. I look at the clock on the stove and see it's only nine a.m.

"Who is it now?" I walk to the front door and open it, only to see my mother on the steps. "Mother?"

"Hi, darling." She sounds cheerful, as if to make a show of how happy she is to see me.

"What are you doing here, Mom?"

"I stopped by to see what you're up to. I hope you don't mind."

"I don't like when you come unannounced." I sound cold and would rather tell her to turn around and leave.

"I'm your mother. I can do whatever I want." She brushes my shoulder and enters the house.

I look at her over my shoulder and watch her look around the house, shocked by how messy and dirty it is.

"I stopped by to see how you're doing, sweetheart."

"I'm fine." I'm short with her. Mother looks at me as if she is studying me. I don't seem like myself since Jake disappeared, she says. I seem easily irritated and rattled and I don't seek company. I don't know what she expects from me. But she wants to hang around me to be my support system. I've told her many times that I need nothing.

Mother has changed beyond all recognition. When Jake was born, she stopped using drugs and never returned to them. She has become a chain smoker, as if that's a consolation prize. She enjoys being a grandmother a lot more than a mother. Perhaps there's a lot more love to give when there is a lot less responsibility attached. Her efforts are endearing, but I find them simply annoying. She now tries to convince me I need to take care of myself, even though she acts and looks like a wreck.

"I'm hoping you and I can go shopping today. You know, we can take a walk to the park and breathe in some fresh air."

I shake my head and wave my hand. "I can't, I'm busy."

"You're busy? What are you doing today to keep busy?"

"Things." I look down at the floor and can't wait for my mother to leave.

"It's not the day for cleaning." Mother looks around the kitchen—the many dirty dishes in the sink, several pots sitting on the stove, the spillage dried out and standing out on the floor. "Do you want me to help you clean?"

"No!" I shoot out. "I mean, I can do it myself, don't worry."

Mother looks as if she's on the verge of crying. Jake's disappearance is difficult for her. He has meant the world to her, her only grandson. When he disappeared, she couldn't sleep, and she's lost weight in a short amount of time. She smells of sweat, and it's obvious she hasn't taken a shower in days. Her hair looks disheveled, and her gray hairs stand out more when dirty.

"I know it's been difficult, sweetheart," Mother says. She maintains a calm voice, something she's learned to do over the years. "And you know we all hope that Jake will turn up someday, but...," she composes herself and stops her eyes from welling up, "but I don't understand any of this. I feel you're not telling me something important."

"I don't know what you're talking about." I sound angry and don't appreciate my mother's accusation. She needs to leave the house before I blow up.

"You're spending too much time alone in this house. How about considering going out with friends?"

"What friends?" When I returned home, Steve invited me out to hang out with his friends from high school several times, but I didn't want to go through the torture. I shake my head in dismissal. "You know I don't have many friends here. Besides, I'm okay, and I don't need your advice, Mom. Give it up!"

Mother looks at me desperately, as if she knows she has lost this battle. The unwelcome aura in the house makes her fidget in her chair until she stands up, ready to leave. "Well, I'll be on my way. Please call me if you need anything. Okay, honey?"

She approaches me while I am still sitting on the chair, motionless, and kisses my forehead. I lift my head and shoot a gaze at my mother. Her blue eyes look empty. Mother flinches and turns around and heads for the door.

"Bye, darling. I will talk to you soon."

As soon as the front door slams, my shoulders relax again. I sigh. If I could only tell her to stop coming unannounced. There's something disrespectful about it.

I go to the bedroom and change into a pair of jeans and a T-shirt. There are dark circles around my eyes when I look in the bedroom mirror. I run over the circles with my hands as if that's going to remove them. Maybe I should put on some makeup to conceal them, but why bother? I'm just going to a grocery store for a quick shopping run and then back home.

I run downstairs and grab the car keys. My blue Ford Pinto is in front of the house. I throw my cell phone to the passenger seat and sit at the steering wheel, tapping my pockets to make sure I didn't forget my wallet. When I turn on the engine, I notice my neighbor Ryan in the distance, standing in front of his house, staring. If my eyes don't fool me, he looks rather inquisitive. I stop paying him any more attention and put my car in reverse. I pull out of my driveway and head in the grocery store's direction.

I enjoy doing grocery shopping when most people consider going to a park or a beach on a perfectly sunny summer day. On a day like this, I'm sure the grocery store would be half-empty. As I turn onto the main street, I turn on the radio and the music plays. It muffles the sounds of the traffic, though, I'm in the mood to listen to music. I turn the station dial to find another station and just as I settle for one, a news announcement comes on.

And now breaking news. As of this morning, a ten-year-old, Brianna Raynolds, is missing. She was last seen at the McKenzie Park. She is four feet and....

I switch the station, abandoning the announcement. What has become of this town with children missing? Is it no longer safe? It wasn't this way when I was growing up.

As I continue driving, I see a man pulled over on the shoulder, looking distressed over his broken-down car. My foot keeps pressing the gas pedal and I pass him. He looks familiar, but I don't bother double checking or pulling over to help.

As I suspected, the grocery store is nearly empty. I take out a list from my pocket and walk down the aisles, locating the items on my list. When I approach the cereal shelf, I see the Lucky Charms Jake loves so much. I place my hand on the box, like an old habit of mine, hold it for a few seconds, then release it, putting it back in its place. Jake ate cereal every morning. He'd put a handful in a bowl of milk, stir it a little, and dig in with a spoon.

I fell into memory lane until a voice behind her startled me. "Sam?"

I gasp. Steve is standing behind me.

"Hey." I say. It is not uncommon to run into someone

you know in this small town. But I wasn't ready to face Steve this morning. "It's good to see you."

A look of empathy encompasses his face. "Hey listen, sorry I didn't call this morning." Steve promised to call every morning and talk to me, whether he has news to share. "We're still investigating Jake's missing case, but as you know, it's been slow. We have had no leads since he disappeared. Trust me, this case is my priority. I've meant to call you and tell you this, but... but it's not the greatest news. I wasn't sure how you'd react."

I look down at the floor like a shy little girl, then up at Steve. "I appreciate that, Steve."

"Hey, listen, there are a few of us getting together this coming Friday. Care to join?"

Here we go again.

"Thanks, Steve, but no."

"If you change your mind, call me."

"Yeah... yeah, will do," I stutter.

"Take care, Sam."

I looked after him as he moves like Terminator with his large muscles. What does he do to maintain them, I wonder?

I walk around the store, feeling all the eyes on me like I was some kind of freak. I pay no one any attention and walk to the register to pay for my items.

On my way home, I stop by a local coffee shop and grab a cup of coffee. I've been sluggish the past few days, and extra coffee is a welcome reprieve for my inertia. When I step into the car, in the corner of my eye, I notice my cell phone light up. I bring it close to me and read the message:

. . .

Sam, I know what you have done.

It's a text from an Unknown Sender.

I put the phone back on the seat, turn on the engine, and take off. As I drive, I am feeling sick to my stomach. Who the hell would send a text like that? Is it someone playing with my mind?

I pull into the house driveway and grab the phone. When I open it, the text has gone. I'm sure I didn't delete it, as I saw the message on the screen without using the password to open my phone. I close the phone and open it again in case it was a glitch. But when I reopen the phone, the only texts I see are from a few days ago, and the latest ones from my mom. Is everything okay?

It is a mystery. Maybe I didn't get the text after all. Was I seeing things after several sleepless nights?

An unsettling feeling follows me around, like someone is watching or stalking me. I take the groceries and enter the house. The dust is visible through the ray of sunshine, giving it a mystic view. The air feels heavy and humid; it's difficult to breathe inside. I secure all the locks and keep the blinds down. I haven't opened the windows in a few days. Darkness envelopes the walls, and the house looks ghostly and uninviting. I step into the middle of the hallway and take a deep breath. This house is old, and it creaks all the time. It was built back in the 1920s and we did very little to it to bring it up to contemporary standards.

The kitchen, like the rest of the house, looks old and unruly. I store the groceries into the refrigerator when, suddenly, a voice behind me startles me. "Mommy."

I scream. "Oh, my God!"

I turn around and see Jake standing in the kitchen. He looks disheveled, his hair messy, his favorite dino T-shirt covered with food, and he stands there, staring at me with his gigantic eyes. "Oh my God, Jake. You scared the shit out of me. What are you doing here?"

"Mommy, I've missed you." His eyes do not blink.

"I've missed you, too, honey."

"What am I doing here right now, Mommy?"

"You're missing. That's what you're doing, honey. Missing."

"How much longer will I be missing, Mommy?" His face expression doesn't change. His eyes remain wide open. His voice is cool and collected. He stands straight like a soldier.

"I don't know, honey. I just don't know."

"Mommy, can we go to a park soon?"

"Maybe, honey. There's a good chance we can."

"Mommy. You look sad. What's wrong?"

I stare in front of me, and drift my hands to my face. My body convulses. I'm sobbing and my screaming bounces off the old kitchen walls.

"Oh my God, oh my God, oh my God. Jake! Jake! What have I done?"

CHAPTER FIFTY-SEVEN

Several news channels report Jake's missing. Every half an hour, between five and seven p.m., his picture covers the TV screen. I sit on the couch and watch my boy's beautiful face. The local and state police are deep in the investigation. The FBI gets involved. My house is a revolving door with different agents visiting and questioning me endlessly until every bit of information can help lead to Jake's finding. Steve is always there, listening in to my conversations with the agents and absorbing every word. He squints his eyes at the mention of Corey. The agents ask me many questions about Jake's father, and I tell them the truth. Corey and I met at a coffee shop and had a short fling. When he got me pregnant, I moved back home to Corey's disliking. He wanted us to live together like a happy family, but I was too young to be tied to one man.

When I said that, I looked at Steve, and he smiled.

The search extends far away, to every corner of the country. When Jake's little face shows up on TV, I am hugging a pillow and listening to every word the news anchor says:

It is now a third day since a four-year-old boy, Jake Crawford, is missing. Last time he was seen was at the community pool in a New Mexico, downtown Gallup. The police authority state that the search is underway with no clear suspects in mind. If you know anything related to the case, please call the number on the screen.

My phone rings. It's my mother. I pick it up and she's crying. "Sam, did you see the news?"

"Mother, yes. I saw the news. The police are doing everything they can to find Jake."

"I miss him, Sam. I miss him so much. I'm praying for him every day and hope he will turn up." My phone beeps, signaling another call. I remove it from my ear to see who is calling. It's Steve.

"Mom, I'm getting another call. I'll call you right back." I hang up the call with my mom and answer Steve's call, sounding gravely depressed and concerned. "Hello?"

"Sam, it's me. Steve."

"I know." Every time Steve wants to discuss Jake's case, I tell him I prefer to do it in the police station or over the phone. It is creepy for me to discuss my son in my home. I find it disrespectful and painful. Steve obeys my wishes, though. He tells me he finds it as strange as it sounds.

"Of course, yes." He clears his throat. "Did you just watch the news?"

"I did." I prefer to stay short with him. Steve is a good guy, and he means well, but he's powerless in a situation like this.

"The entire country has been on the move to find

Jake. But I wanted to talk to you about something else. Can you meet me somewhere?"

"What is there to talk about, Steve?"

"I wanted to talk about Jake's father. It's not a conversation I want to have over the phone. When can you meet me?"

I roll my eyes at the sound of this. But I play along, because I don't want to sounds elusive as to raise any suspicion.

I agree to meet Steve in a cozy dive bar in Gallup, a couple of miles from my house. The bar is the place we often visited after school—our mutual friend Al knew the owner who allowed the high school youngsters to drink underage. It was no surprise, because the owner carefully curated the place for the local drunks who found solace in the bar.

It is an early Sunday evening when Steve and I meet—I didn't think the bar would have any visitors then, as was the case back in our high school days—but I'm wrong. A couple of out-of-town fellows are sitting at the bar, watching the TV overhead. I see Michelle's ghost dancing as a shadow on the wall, and I don't mind. Her shadow makes me miss her. I smile.

When Steve enters the bar and sees me, he gives me a big hug and a kiss on my cheek. He sits on the chair across. His usual cheerful demeanor changes to a quiet and pensive one. "How are you holding up?" he asks.

"Okay." I answer with no emotion added. I feel depleted.

"It's good to see you again." Steve puts a soft smile on his face. "I wish the circumstances were different." I nod my head and look down at the table.

"Do you want something to drink?" He points his index finger at me. I take a few seconds to think.

"A glass of water is fine."

He stands up and walks to the bar, as there are no waitresses in a tiny place like this one. He orders himself a shot of whiskey and a glass of water for me. I look at my watch to see what time it is—hopefully he's done with his shift for the day. I can't picture him running after a thief under the influence. Though, with his large stature, I'd imagine he'd need a lot more than a single shot to get drunk.

He sits down, raises his glass, and swallows the whiskey in one gulp. I take my glass of water and sip it slowly while watching Steve grimace over the glass rim.

"This shit is good," he says.

"What did you want to talk about, Steve?" I cut to the chase.

"The search for Jake is ongoing. I get the police reports every day and I read them carefully. No one has reported a missing child. Not a word or a hint of where he might be. We suspect that he might have been taken to another state, or even another country, so the search might need to expand."

I remain silent and stare at him.

"The only suspect we have right now is his father, though we have no evidence of his involvement at all. He's being investigated and we're trying to get clues about his whereabouts, but it's been a tough mission so far."

"Sounds reassuring," I whisper.

"I promise we will find Jake. We believe he's still alive and out there. It's just a matter of time when we will find him."

I sigh in relief. "None of you think he's... dead, do

you?" I swallow a clump in my throat, as I picture Jake lying lifeless somewhere in a ditch along the road.

Steve slowly shakes his head while staring at me. "Unlikely. We searched every corner of this county the day he disappeared. He would have been found by now." Steve leans forward and nearly whispers, "Can you tell me more about his father?"

"I've already shared everything." At first, I sound defensive, so I soften my voice. "I can't think of any other information to share."

"I don't believe you've told me everything, Sam. I think you're hiding something. You better say it all before the FBI discovers it. As your friend, I don't want you to get into trouble."

Maybe Steve isn't as dumb as I think.

"How dare you! My son is missing, and you think I'd be hiding things from you. Why would I do that, Steve?"

He shrugs and tilts his head. "I don't know. I just find it peculiar that you don't know your son's father's last name. Things don't add up, Sam. Tell me everything."

"What are you trying to get at?" My voice comes out more harshly than I wanted. I clench my fist and I feel like storming out of the bar, but that would make things much worse for me.

"Nothing." He gives his hand a wave. "I'm sorry. I'm just a little stressed out from all this. I don't mean to interrogate you, I promise." He reaches for my hand, but I yank it out of his way.

"Then don't." I can't help it. I stand up and storm out of the bar, leaving Steve behind.

CHAPTER FIFTY-EIGHT

Ever since the cops got involved in the investigation, my life got a lot more uncomfortable. I was under the microscope all the time, as if I were the suspect. On day ten of Jake's missing, they patrolled and came to visit less and less. Still, no leads revealed where Jake could be. They have not found Corey yet either. The local TV and radio stations gave up on sharing the news about the missing boy. It was as if a mystery no longer held interest, as there were no clues to use in its untangling.

My mother keeps acting like a nervous wreck. Ever since Jake disappeared, she visits her church and prays every day. On her way back from church, she calls me and tells me that Jake is alive. God has spoken to her, she says. She stops by every other day and brings a casserole of food for us to share. She needs company. Her eyes have sunk deeper into her sockets, her hair looks disheveled, making her look older. All this eats away at her, and she keeps reassuring herself that Jake was indeed alright, and that he would turn up one day.

But every time she shows up at my door, I scold her. "Mom. Please stop bringing me food. I'm not hungry."

"Sweetheart, you need to eat," she says tearfully as she walks through the door.

"Mom, listen." I say. "I know you're sad about Jake, and so am I, but your constant crying and moaning are not helping me. We need to be clearheaded."

She wipes her tears and looks at me. "Yes, you're right. We need to stay strong." She keeps her eyes on me and asks, "What about you? Every time I come here, you look nervous. What's going on?"

Her question feels like a punch in the stomach. "What do you mean? I'm not nervous. It's just that your crying is getting on my nerves."

"How dare you?" She raises her voice. "You're acting like everything's fine, and nothing is! Don't you tell me again to stop crying. I won't stand for your foolish advice."

"Suit yourself." I turn around and walk away. She stands behind me and mumbles something to herself. Then I hear the door slam—my mother has left the house, bringing me instant relief.

I walk into Jake's room to sort his toys and put them in the bin where he has curated a selection of his favorites. A bright-green turtle stands out against the other toys, and I take it in my hands and rub it against my cheek. "Oh, Jake. My little sunshine."

I lie on the floor until the darkness outside lulls me to sleep.

At three in the morning, I hear a loud thump. I can't tell if the noise is coming from inside or outside, but then I hear a scream. "Mommy, Mommy."

It sounds like Jake. He sounds sweet and innocent. I

wonder what he's doing so early in the morning. I prop myself up against the floor and run toward the front door. When I open it, my screams reach the neighborhood. "Jake, Jake, where are you? Come back!"

But no one hears me; no one reacts.

I walk through the porch and around the house, and look for Jake, but he is nowhere. The darkness there looks deep and scary. A cloud hides the moon. The house gives no light reflection; the window blinds conceal any life inside. I only hear crickets and feel the sultry summer air. I run back and trip on a tree branch. The branch splits in half. My right ankle feels sore, but I keep going.

Inside the house, I rummage through the rooms, looking for Jake. I scream, "Jake, where are you? Everything will be alright, my boy. Hang in there!"

Out of nowhere, Jake finally appears. He stands in the hallway, with arms hung along his body. "Mommy, I'm here. Let's go to bed now." He smiles.

CHAPTER FIFTY-NINE

The next thing I know, I'm lying in my bed in my day clothes. I look at the clock on the dresser and see it's nine. My memory of climbing into the bed last night is faint. Outside, the rain is beating the ground with vengeance. I welcome the reprieve from the hot days. A sharp pain in my head feels like a knife stabbing me. It's been a while since I had a migraine. I stand up and put the shades up on the windows and go back to bed. I hope some light will ease my headache. The day looks dark, and removing the blinds doesn't make any difference. I close my eyes and doze off.

I don't know how much time passes before my phone rings. I let it go to voicemail, but the phone rings again.

Removing the cover from my head, I peek at my phone next to me and see Steve's name on the screen.

"Hello?" My voice sounds coarse.

"Sam, we must talk. There are some developments in Jake's father's search. You must come see me. I'm at the police station."

Like a cloud disappearing and exposing the sun, this news brightens my day. The migraine now feels miniscule.

"Let me get ready, and I'll see you soon."

I put clothes on and head to the kitchen. Like every day, I fill two bowls of cereal, add milk—a little extra in one, just like Jake likes—eat mine, and head through the door.

Driving to the station, I swirl around to avoid large potholes filled with rain. As if God is angry, the drops are making loud noises. The rain is faster than the windshield wipers can remove it.

Against the dark sky, the police station looks gray. Several police cars are parked in the front. I put the hood on to protect myself from the rain and fasten my steps to the station door. As soon as I enter, silence takes over the space—a bold difference from the raging rain outside. No one sits at the front desk. From a corner, Steve peeks his head and signals me with his hand to come on over. He turns around and I follow him, hoping the good news is awaiting.

We enter his office, which smells of fresh donuts and coffee. He sits down and instructs me to the do the same.

When he takes a better look at me, he exclaims, "You're soaked!"

"It's pouring outside."

"I love it when it rains. People are much less motivated to commit crimes in shitty weather." He smiles, and I say nothing and wait for Steve to deliver the news. He gazes at me with a stern look, studying my face expression. I am growing inpatient, but I would never let Steve see that. He finally speaks. "The state of California has discovered some interesting facts about Jake's father."

I smile inside, and I'm eager to hear the news. It sounds the FBI, or whoever, has made progress. My well-crafted plan seems to have worked so far. Steve leans against the chair, furrowing his brow. I gaze at his coffee cup on the table, then and back at his eyes. He looks concerned or surprised. It's difficult to tell which.

"First off, Corey is not his real name." I flinch. This piece of news is unexpected. In retrospect, of course, it makes sense. I wonder if Michael is really Michael, if Shauna is Shauna, and if Brian is Brian. I now doubt it. I don't let my anger reveal my surprise. My poker face is intact. "The man in question, Jake's father, was born James David Smith."

"Oh." I say, my heart beating fast.

"I suppose you wouldn't have known that. Or did you?"

"No." I shake my head. "Definitely not."

He leans forward while keeping his gaze on me. "Have you told me everything about Jake's father, Sam? I'm asking you one more time."

My leg is fidgeting out of nervousness, because I know Steve suspects something. I stop it and take a calm stance. I regret underestimating Steve. I continue to play along with my story. "Yes. Yes, everything I know. Why would I hide things?"

"Because some things are not adding up. I feel you might have bent the truth a bit about this man."

"But why would I do that? I have no reason to hide anything. He kidnapped Jake, and I'm desperate for you to find him."

"Well, here's the thing. The private detective we hired has found Corey—or should I say James—and he has kept a close eye on him. There are no traces of Jake anywhere.

Corey may no longer be our prime suspect in this case, though unfortunately for him, other facts have resurfaced during this case search."

"What did they find?" I say, eager to hear the answer.

He nods. "And I suppose you weren't aware that he is a mastermind for human trafficking?"

I first widened my eyes in shock, but they narrow at Steve's question. I tilt my head. "Now, why would I know that, Steve? That's quite a disturbing thing to say."

"I'm not accusing you of anything, Sam. This complete story is missing a puzzle. I only hope that you're not involved in human trafficking. Are you?"

"Steve, you're out of your mind. What prompts you to say this?"

"If I can be honest, you don't strike me as someone who enjoys being a single mother. I've seen you around the kid—you look miserable. You know, you're young, beautiful. I presume your dream of becoming an actress is still brewing inside you."

"Stop it now, Steve."

He stares at me, and swirls in his chair left to right, and repeats. I can feel he wants to instigate, but he doesn't.

"Okay." He lifts his right palm and dunks his head. "I won't be speculating anymore. But know Corey is still under a close investigation and when we find enough evidence of his human trafficking activities, he will be arrested."

"He will?" I say. It's what I've wanted all along.

He nods. "You better believe it. As for Jake." He shakes his head and closes his eyes. After a few seconds, he opens them with a tear on the side of each. "We will keep searching. Though it has been hopeless."

I dunk my head and stare down at my feet. The pain of the teeth penetrating the skin is what I feel when I bite down on my lower lip. I look up at Steve and said, "If Corey didn't kidnap Jake, then who did?"

CHAPTER SIXTY

Everyone in the town knows about Jake missing. People I haven't spoken to in years drop by to offer a word of consolation. They ask if I need anything to get by. I stand on the porch, arms crossed, and with tears in my eyes, thanking them for being a good neighbor. The town churches call for a prayer for Jake after the Sunday mass. The people at the pews look down ahead and whisper the prayers. My mother interrupts it with her loud wail and all eyes rest on her. Why haven't they found Jake already? Where could he be? Is he safe?

Could Jake be dead?

On one Sunday, I feel bold enough to talk to my mother. I want to reveal my secret. It might have been cruel to think this, but I want her to be distracted. To hear something shocking that she can ruminate over. She has lost noticeable weight since Jake's missing, and she looks ghostly. If I didn't want to see her before because of her constant nagging, now I don't want to see her to watch the sad display of my mother's body declining. I put my hand on her shoulder when the mass is over, and whisper in her ear, "Mom, let's go home."

She takes me under the arm and we walk down the aisle like I am hauling an aged, disabled woman. The people offer their condolences as if Jake is already gone. I whisper to Mother, "Mom, don't listen to them. They don't have faith like we do."

My mother gives a slight nod and continues walking with her head down.

I usher her to my car and rush over to the driver's side to let her in and take her home. On our way there, I check her face once in a while. Her eyes now have deep circles and her hair has grayed.

"Mom, we need to talk." She stares ahead and doesn't say a word. "Mom?"

Like she's just been awoken, she stirs up a bit and says, "Yes. What do you want to talk about?"

"Not here. When we come home."

She irons her skirt with her hand and sniffles a couple of times.

"Okay," she says.

"Are you hungry?"

Shaking her head, she says, "No, I'm not."

"Mom, you need to eat. You're getting skinny. Should we stop somewhere to get a sandwich? A pizza maybe?"

"No, no. Just keep driving, dear."

We spend the rest of the ride in dead silence. We pull into the driveway and Mother lights a cigarette as soon as she touches the ground. She has chain-smoked for weeks to calm her nerves. I don't appreciate her smoking around the house, but I say nothing. She has experienced enough.

I wait for her on the porch. She's facing her back to me. Her body looks smaller and weak.

She flicks the cigarette butt into the air and we walk inside the house, appreciating the old scenery. I take two glasses out of the kitchen cabinet and pour orange juice. We sit at the kitchen table, my mother looking at one spot. She walks her fingers to the glass and takes it to her lips to taste the juice. I seek a perfect minute to say what had been on my mind for days, for months, for years. A knot forms in my stomach. I take a deep breath.

"Mom, there's something I've been meaning to tell you for a long time now." I release a breath, dreading what is to come. "This won't be easy to talk about."

"What is it?" Worry covers her face.

"I've been guilty about this ever since it happened." I clench my fists, look down at the floor, and raise my head to see a tearful mother. "I don't know how else to say this. But... I was the one who killed Father."

"Oh. Darling." She stands from her chair and comes to me to give me a hug. My arms hang against my body on the sides. She releases me from her hug and looks at me. "Darling, darling. Why would you say that?"

"Because... because I did. He lost control of the wheel and drove into a building after I knocked him with a hard object while he was driving. I didn't mean to, but I did. I killed him, Mom. Please forgive me."

She shakes her head. "No, no, you didn't. Dad didn't die in the car accident, darling. They took him to the hospital, still alive. His injury was minimal, but they kept him in the hospital overnight after they ran blood tests. The following day, he died of a heart attack."

"What? That can't be right."

Mother shakes her head and confirms, "It can be and it is."

"Mom, I killed Dad. He made your life miserable. He had to go." I scream.

"No, Sam. That's not true. Dad didn't make my life miserable. He was one of the kindest people I've known, and he loved you very much. I was heartbroken when he died."

"That can't be. He was brutal to both of us."

"Oh, dear Sam. Father was heartbroken after he lost his parents. But he never treated us poorly. I think your memory is distorted, sweetheart."

I place my left hand on my waist while I tangle the right one in my hair. "Fuck." I say. Then more words spew from my mouth, "Fuck, fuck, fuck, fuck."

My mother tilts her head, looking sad for me. "Did you think you killed Dad this whole time? Did you live with this guilt your whole life, dear?" She opens up her arms. "Come to Mother. I knew all along something had to be wrong."

CHAPTER SIXTY-ONE

A strange feeling comes over me after my mother has revealed the cause of Father's death. Betrayal has replaced the guilt that permeated deep into my soul. Everything I have believed, am guilty of, is a fat lie. I jump in the car and endlessly drive around the neighborhood. The dusk is peeking its head over the horizon. I take a right and remember to take a long, windy road I have not been on in years. The road is desolate. I turn on the radio to listen to a local station. News is on. A weather forecast. Happenings around the world. Interesting bits and tips. Nothing about Jake. Like he never existed.

I take a narrow road that leads to the cemetery. Vegetation improves immediately, as if fed by the resting souls. I drive around, trying to recall where my father was buried. Last time I was here was for my father's funeral. I was six years old, and my memory has faded since then. All I remember is that my mother insisted we bury him next to the grandparents who we'd lost two years prior to father's death. The cemetery is empty except for the two cars seeking their final destination. In the middle of a field, a willow tree draws my immediate attention.

"Hm. This tree was here before," I whisper.

I park on the path and look at what's in front of me. That has to be the location. Though the tree looks more mature, sadder. I get out of the car and take small steps toward the cluster of graves. Memories are coming back. I see my mother all over again, standing above the coffin and crying. I remember feeling numb, yet guilty for being unable to cry. To express sadness about my father's passing. There weren't as many people at his funeral as my grandparents'. Father had made a few enemies in town and was ousted by a few circles.

I remember Michelle and her mother standing across from me. Michelle had looked at me with sad eyes, giving a small wave. I smiled at her, and she smiled back. When they placed the coffin deep in the ground, my mother wailed.

I walk closer to where the tree sits and look around. There, in one spot, lie three tombstones, similar in size and shape. The grass covers the ground, making them look abandoned. The one on the right is my father's. I kneel to the ground and read the stone.

WILLIAM RICHARD CRAWFORD
1963-2004
REST IN PEACE

A breeze caresses my face. It's getting darker outside. I sit akimbo on the ground and stare at the letters shaped into my father's name. This is the first time I've visited his grave after he died, even though I have passed by the main road zillion times. It has been difficult to face him.

To unburden my guilt.

Calm comes over me, and I fix my eyes on the stone. I want to talk to him; to see him one last time. Maybe he can hear me?

"Dad," I begin. "Mom told me how you died. Ugh. I'm such a moron. This whole time, for over fifteen years, I thought I was the one who killed you. Sometimes, I prayed for your forgiveness, and even though you might have granted it, I couldn't live at peace."

I stop to reevaluate my speech. Is he listening? I am certain he is.

"I don't think I'm a bad person, Dad. Do you?" I let out a small laugh, realizing he can't answer. "Life is strange. Really strange. I got in trouble with a small group of criminals. I was fooled into believing them, and I'm so ashamed."

I rock on the ground, back and forth, to reposition myself.

"But, you know what? As much as guilt got me paralyzed, I ended up fighting them back." I am pleased with this thought, and I smile. I pluck a string of grass from the ground and chew on it. The bitterness of it makes me discard it. "I think I'm going to win this one. I'm an excellent actress, Dad. You'd be proud. Real proud." I turn around to notice a car passing by. The driver looks at me and I wave. The car disappears from my sight, and I turn to my father.

"Dad, I have a grave secret." My heart is pounding and I feel my palms sweat. "But I don't know how I should feel about it. I don't know if I've made the right decision." A tear trickles down my cheek. "I hope all is going to be over soon. Dad, I'm a monster. I'm a monster. A monster! Can you hear me?"

My sobs replace my words.

CHAPTER SIXTY-TWO

My mouth is agape as I watch Corey walking out of the big house with his hands handcuffed on his back. He's hiding his face from the cameras. Cops hold him on each side. The cul-de-sac is full of police cars and news reporters, and in the middle, Corey's white BMW. The lawn on which I once stood is blocked off by the yellow tape. It looks like a murder scene. I imagine Corey rotting in prison and feel huge relief. I grab a pillow from the couch and beat it like a drum while letting out peals of uproarious laughter.

He got me, but I got him too.

A car pulls into my driveway. It's Steve. With an urgent force, he slides out of his car and knocks on the door, shouting my name. I open the door and see Steve, distressed and standing on my porch.

"Hey," I say.

"Let me in."

I move to the side and let Steve walk through the door. Judging by his face expression and the tone of his voice, he's not here for a happy reason. He sees the TV is on and surmises I knew Corey has been arrested. He ignores the TV and turns to me. I notice a pistol hanging from his belt. His cop uniform looks tight, and his muscles are pronounced.

"I've been calling you all afternoon. Why didn't you pick up?"

"Oh, sorry. I was busy." I touch my nose and put my hand down. "Do you want something to drink? I can make you some coffee."

He shakes his head and says, "Were you watching the news?"

"I saw. I'm relieved," I say. I mean it.

"It is crazy." He pauses as if he was thinking. "Sam, I'm here to warn you. Jake is nowhere to be found and if they do not tie the case to James, I'm afraid you will be the next suspect. If there's anything you're hiding, you better tell me now."

My palms are sweaty. I close my eyes in order to concentrate. I shake my head and look at Steve. "I… there is nothing to say."

Steve follows the path of my eyes as I look around the house. He seems suspicious of my behavior and studies me.

"Sam. Have you ever been in that house?" He points at the TV and refers to James's house shown minutes before.

I shake my head. "No. No, Steve. I've told you everything I knew about James."

Steve walks around the room and listens to potential sounds. I rub my hands together and interrupt him. "Do you want to have a seat?" I turn around and go to the kitchen at the far end of the house. Steve follows me and sits on a chair at the kitchen table. He looks around and grimaces. The kitchen is in complete disarray and I can tell he's disgusted by what he sees. He looks me straight in the eye.

"The police read your report from the day Jake went missing. They went to the swimming pool you took Jake to and asked for surveillance camera footage on the day Jake disappeared."

I stay calm, but a storm is brewing inside me.

Steve puts his hand on the table and taps it with his fingers. He furrows his brows, and anger flashes from his eyes. "They looked through every single detail of the video and they didn't see Jake in it."

I stand in the kitchen motionless and watch Steve's eyes turn darker. He is below my eye level, yet I still feel powerless.

"Things are not looking good for you, Sam. They're thinking that you have something to do with Jake's missing. It's only a matter of time before they come and interrogate you."

I nod and say nothing. Steve stands up and heads for the door. He doesn't turn around, but he keeps talking. "Don't say I didn't warn you. I still care about you, Sam."

He doesn't say goodbye. He walks through the door and rushes to his car.

———

That day, the total fiasco makes the national news: Corey's operation is completely busted. Everyone, including Brian and Michael, Shauna, Leslie, have all been arrested. They have tied Brian's business, Spy Café, as the hub for finding victims. Apparently, in their confession to the police, Corey and Michael have impregnated nineteen women. They sold the babies to families from all over the world who couldn't conceive children of their own. For hefty fees. Of those women, ten were homeless and were murdered after giving birth. The FBI found the remains in the backyard. Nine were set free, though. They were not considered suspects in the operation.

I sigh with relief at all the good news. Corey, Michael and Brian are going to rot in prison, and that is all I wanted.

I pick up the phone and call Mom.

"Yes?"

"Mom, did you see the news today?"

"What news?"

"They've caught everyone in Corey's circle. It's all over, Mom."

"No, it's not," my mother says. "Not until they find Jake."

"Mom?"

"Yes, Sam?"

"Do you mind coming over? I need to go to the police station and see Steve."

My mother doesn't ask questions and says she will be there in fifteen minutes.

CHAPTER SIXTY-THREE

It's time to make the move. I hang up the phone with Mom and I stand up from the couch. I walk through the hallway until I reach the basement door. The key is in my shoe, and I grab it. My right hand is shaking, and I stop it with my left hand. The basement is the place Michelle and I hid as kids during our games. A reminder of what a childhood could be.

At the far corner, where it's darkest, comes the sound of a fan. As I approach it, I notice the covers on the mattress bundled up. They look damp from the mold. Under the covers, a curl of hair is sticking out. I lift the covers to find him lying there, sleeping like an angel. I wake him up out of excitement and hold him in my arms. "Jake, Jake. Wake up, sweetheart."

Jake looks at me, half-asleep, still grasping what's going on, what I am doing there.

"What's going on, Mom?" His sweet voice is soothing. My heart is bursting with joy, happiness, anxiety all at once.

I kiss his cheeks, attempting to get the words out of my mouth. "We're free at last. No one is after us anymore."

I pick him up and carry him upstairs. His arms hang around my neck. He gives me a smile and squeezes me tighter.

"Does that mean I can go to the park and play with my friends?"

I look at him and smile. "Yes, honey. You'll be going to the park and anywhere else you wish. We might even make a trip to Disneyland this year."

"Disneyland!" He perks up and claps his hands. "When can we go, Mom?"

"Soon, honey. Soon." I put him on the couch and bundle him up in the blankets. "Why don't you keep sleeping, love? Do you want some milk?"

He gives two quick nods and draws the blanket closer to his chin.

"I'll be right back." I walk to the kitchen and feel his eyes following me. As I pour milk into Jake's cup, I realize it is time. Time to confess everything. Time to reveal the whole truth.

When I return to the living room, Jake is asleep. Ever since I started keeping him locked in the basement, his energy has been sparse. He's slept a lot and didn't seem like himself. The basement hasn't changed since my grandparents bought the house, but I didn't have any other choice.

His arms are resting on his torso as he falls back to sleep. I wonder if he's having pleasant dreams. I wonder if this chapter of his life will be stored deep in his mind or discarded forever.

Jake is my world. He is my everything.

I pull my phone from my jeans pocket, find Steve's name, and dial. It rings twice until Steve picks it up and says, "Hello?"

"Hi, Steve." I sound as pleasant as I can be. The nerves are getting to me, but I stand proud and dignified. "We need to talk."

"Yes, Sam, we sure do."

"I'm ready to confess everything."

And so I do—I confess everything.

My mother arrives at the house twenty minutes after I call her and when she sees Jake lying on the couch, she screams. She grabs Jake and starts kissing him. Still half-asleep, his grandmother's reaction startles Jake, but he seems happy to see her. For him, everything seems normal.

Mother doesn't let Jake go. She caresses him, plants kisses on his cheeks and cries.

I take a slow ride to the police station and look for Steve when I arrive. He's sitting in his office with another cop, a colleague of his. They both look at me through narrowed eyes. Steve's face is contorted with anger. I stand at the door, smiling, though I can tell they don't appreciate my smile.

"Jake is alive. He's with me." These are the first words I say.

"We suspected so," Steve's colleague says. He seems annoyed by my casual delivery.

"Is your boy okay?" Steve says.

"He's fine." I say, even though I question what spending time in the basement and not seeing a daylight for weeks will do to him. I will think of his recovery later. "I'm here to tell you the entire story."

I sit down and begin. I tell them Brian employed me as a barista at Spy Café. That I fell in lust with Corey. Actually, I don't think I said "in lust." I toned it down, as I could never admit falling for a criminal anymore. I might have said "had a crush," or "took an interest in him," but what was most important was that they believed me, even though Steve scoffed when I said it. All the details of my captivity in L.A. I tell them.

I tell them I made an exchange deal with Corey, that he'd get me an acting gig, and I would give him the baby. That was the exchange we shook on. But I wasn't convinced I wanted someone else to take charge of my child's life. I acted as best as I could—acting was my forte, after all—and pretended I would follow through with the deal. I tell them I unearthed the human remains in the backyard and how I escaped shortly after, and it amazed them to hear it was that simple. "It wasn't simple," I tell them. It sounds simple now, but then, it was one of the hardest things I've ever done in life.

"And faking Jake's kidnapping. What was that all about?" Steve asks.

"Corey had found us a few days prior, and it scared me to death. They threatened to kill me if I told anyone about their human trafficking business. I wanted to take things in my hands. I knew they wanted Jake, but since his disappearance was all over the news, I was hoping they'd leave us alone. And they did. Having Corey as the prime suspect would have led to the uncovering of his operation. And it all worked out."

Steve comes up to me and tells me to put my hands up.

"Samantha Crawford, you are under arrest for a misdemeanor." He clears his throat. "You should never lie to cops, you know. Never." As he handcuffs me, he looks up and gazes at me. "Well, there's no doubt you'll make a superb actress someday."

I smile and extend my arms. I knew this was coming.

CHAPTER SIXTY-FOUR

The judge sentenced me to one year in prison for misleading the investigation in the kidnapping case of my son. I call it good acting. My sentence was with a chance for parole. While I spent time in jail, my mother took care of Jake, and both came to visit every week. I reminded my mother not to smoke in front of my child, and then she broke the news that she had quit for good. Cold turkey.

A little over eight months later, I'm let out early for good behavior. My mother broke the lease of her apartment in Gallup and has moved back into her old home, our house, and helped us pay for the utilities. My acting career is still on hold, but at the forefront of my mind. I no longer have visions or hear voices. But sometimes, years later, whenever Jake has a new life struggle, I advise him, "Perish or persist, young man. You will know when that voice tells you to fight."

THANK YOU!

I sincerely thank you for reading this book!

Please consider leaving a review, even if it's only a sentence, checking out my other books, and subscribing to my website. I'm also happy to answer any questions you may have, so do please get in touch with me via my website:

https://nadijamujagic.com

ABOUT THE AUTHOR

Nadija Mujagić was born and raised in Sarajevo, Bosnia and Herzegovina, what used to be the former Yugoslavia back in the late 1970s. In 1997, she moved to the United States shortly after the end of the Bosnian War and has lived in Massachusetts since. In her spare time, she enjoys playing sports and electric bass guitar. "The Exchange" is her fifth book.

ALSO BY NADIJA MUJAGIC

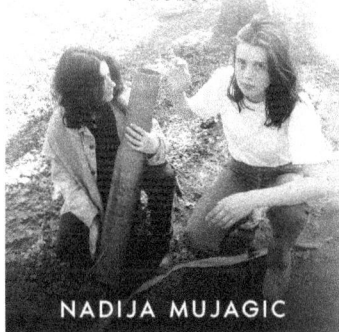

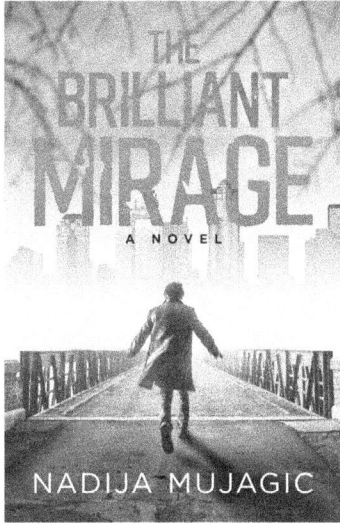